THE MARKETING TOOLKIT

THE MARKETING TOOLKIT

Bite-sized wisdom – perfect for busy people who would sooner be succeeding, not reading

Jeff Della Mura

Viva Books

New Delhi | Mumbai | Chennai | Kolkata | Bengaluru | Hyderabad | Kochi | Guwahati

First Indian Edition 2010

VIVA BOOKS PRIVATE LIMITED

- 4737/23 Ansari Road, Daryaganj, New Delhi 110 002
  E-mail: vivadelhi@vivagroupindia.net, Tel. 42242200
- 76, Service Industries, Shirvane, Sector 1, Nerul, Navi Mumbai 400 706
  E-mail: vivamumbai@vivagroupindia.net, Tel. 27721273, 27721274
- Jamals Fazal Chambers, 26 Greams Road, Chennai 600 006
  E-mail: vivachennai@vivagroupindia.net, Tel. 28290304, 28294241
- B-103, Jindal Towers, 21/1A/3 Darga Road, Kolkata 700 017
  E-mail: vivakolkata@vivagroupindia.net, Tel. 22836381, 22816713
- 7, Sovereign Park Apartments, 56-58, K. R. Road, Basavanagudi, Bengaluru 560 004
  E-mail: vivabangalore@vivagroupindia.net, Tel. 26607409, 26607410
- 101-102 Mughal Marc Apartments, 3-4-637 to 641, Narayanguda, Hyderabad 500 029
  E-mail: vivahyderabad@vivagroupindia.net, Tel. 27564481, 27564482
- Beevi Towers, First Floor, SRM Road, Kaloor, Kochi 682 018, Kerala
  E-mail: vivakochi@vivagroupindia.net, Tel: 0484-2403055, 2403056
- 232, GNB Road, Beside UCO Bank, Silpukhuri, Guwahati 781 003
  E-mail: vivaguwahati@vivagroupindia.net, Tel: 0361-2666386

www.vivagroupindia.com

Published by arrangement with
How to Books
Spring Hill House, Spring Hill Road
Begbroke, Oxford OX5 1RX,
United Kingdom

NOTE: The material contained in this book is set out in good faith for general guidance and no liability can be accepted for loss or expense incurred as a result of relying in particular circumstances on statements made in the book. The laws and regulations are complex and liable to change, and readers should check the current position with the relevant authorited before making personal arrangements.

ISBN : 978-81-309-1457-2

Published by Vinod Vasishtha for Viva Books Private Limited, 4737/23, Ansari Road, New Delhi-110 002. Printed and bound by Swan Press, New Delhi.

M0000 / M0245

Contents

Acknowledgements

This book would not exist at all but for the support of three people. Firstly, Patrick Forsyth whose wisdom and unselfish advice helped me to find the right publisher. Secondly, Nikki Read at How to Books for proving to be exactly the right publisher. And thirdly, my wife, Tina, who has patiently administered the fallout that an undertaking such as this will create.

I am also indebted to the small army of luminaries, professionals, colleagues and friends who have kindly given their time and expertise in helping to ensure that the contents of this book are appropriate and worthwhile. I am especially grateful to the following for their notable contributions. In no particular order or categorisation, I wish to thank: Professor Malcolm McDonald; Professor Alan Wilson; Lynda Purser – Director of the Institute of Business Consulting; Andrew Chalk of the Chartered Institute of Marketing's small business group; Denise Rossiter of Essex Chambers of Commerce; Claire Lindsay and Julie Jones at the University of Essex; Graham Lowing at Wordsworth PR; Dr Brian D Smith; Terry Taber of The Federation of Small Businesses; Mac and Annie York; Tom and Phyllis Laurence of Delgat Data Entry; author Heather White at the Magic of Networking; Thorsten Klein and Adrian Birtwell at the University of East London; Paul del Bianco; Steve and Denise at Leo Print; Paul Weeks – Senior Lecturer at Ashcroft International Business School, Anglia Ruskin University; Andy at Griib Design; Karon Clark at Epic Telemarketing; Jas Bains of Cooney Bains; Paul Narraway of MDI Sales Performance; Ian Buzer of www.preloved.co.uk; Phil Hitchman; Paula Della Mura; Sam Morris; Clare Parker; Emma Healey at The Chartered Institute of Marketing – Essex Branch; Struan Robertson – technology lawyer at Pinsent Masons; Chris and Louise Della Mura; Caroline Bartlett at The Atrium Clinic; Dr Barry Ardley at Lincoln Business School, The University of Lincoln; assorted colleagues at Business Link, East of England especially Stuart Keppie and Nicholas Wilkinson; Paul Stafford at Newman & Partners; and finally Dr Jakob Nielsen of the Nielsen Norman Group USA.

Thank you and bless you all.

Foreword

by Patrick Forsyth

Marketing matters

Marketing is a complex business. If resources are tight – as they often are in small and medium sized organisations – then it can be difficult to fit in, yet some ad hoc approaches that appear to make marketing action easier, less expensive and quicker can cause grave problems. As this book could be well described as an antidote to such approaches, setting out as it does clear guidelines designed to prompt practical, useful and effective action, perhaps getting the 'what not to do' aspect out of the way is a reasonable approach to a Foreword and to put readers in a constructive frame of mind to appreciate the rest of this book.

Marketing can be simplistically described as activity to bring in the business, it needs to be done effectively yet is rarely said to be easy. Marketing activity must be customer-focused, continuously deployed, creatively originated and deployed and a complex mix of activity organised and co-ordinated. It needs planning and a systematic approach, it needs . . . Enough. Surely there must be some straightforward approaches?

There are, of course (this book is full of them) but here my intention is to show the danger of pursuing what appears to be a 'quick fix'; approaches that seem all too easy when budgets and time are under pressure. Several approaches, chosen as most commonly observed, can, in fact, cause problems.

Danger ahead

All the following might be described as forms of 'ad hoc' marketing. Such approaches include:

- **Doing something only when there is time**: when workload permits do some marketing. But marketing activity must fit not *your* timing, but that inherent in the market and with customers. Failing to maintain continuity can quickly lead to so-called 'feast and famine':

a situation with which many small firms are familiar. As a result, one minute there can be no prospects to follow and convert, the next – after a burst of activity – there can be too many simultaneous leads to deal with properly.

- **Convenient action**: activities favoured because of some particular factor which makes them convenient – *Mary's got some free time this week, let's get her on the telephone to a few people.* Mary may not be up to it, and the telephone may not be the best form of contact.
- **Subcontracting**: in other words, selecting marketing activity that you can get someone else to do. This seems easy, and is also easy to decide (everyone votes for something that will not involve *them* in any personal hassle). A quarterly newsletter that can be produced externally, perhaps by a public relations consultancy, is a good example. Many companies have got locked into producing such a thing, rejoiced that it is easy to do, then found that it does not produce good returns.
- **Familiarity**: just because you may be good at something does not make it first choice for use. For example, a financial services firm stopped using cartoons on their promotional material after research showed that their clients viewed them as frivolous and inappropriate; much to the disappointment of the member of staff who loved drawing them.
- **On offer**: for example in advertising. One firm of printers recently told me that almost all their promotional budget for the year had been spent progressively as magazines telephoned them – *we have a special feature on promotional print and all your competitors are taking space.* Some of this was no doubt useful, but the ideal mix demanded more.
- **What is fashionable:** this is a form of copycat action and is never to be recommended (of course you can copy or adapt methodology, but there should always be reason for it beyond simply viewing it as good 'because XYZ does it'). For example, how many accountants manage to make their budget briefings truly different from those of their competitors? Hardly a sign of original thinking.
- **Perpetuating the same action**: sometimes a good idea continues in use beyond its sell-by date as it were, for no other reason than that it has become familiar and thus easy. Given a choice between more of the same and taking time to adapt or innovate, more of the same wins, and wins again, until method is stale and results confirm this. The antithesis of this can pay dividends.

- **Action unsupported by appropriate skills**: if the personal skills that are involved are inadequate to the task then any good will be, at the least, diluted. For example, I recently attended the Budget Briefing of a local firm of accountants. Such events can work well and are well proven – but the poor standard of presentation (and lack of interest it sparked in the audience) negated any good effect. Similarly, a letter that I recently received was written personally. It contained an apology (don't ask) and made sales points for the future. But it was so strikingly old-fashioned and full of *officespeak* as to negate its message entirely.

- **Panic action**: this is never a good idea. If sales drop or competition increases and urgent action is required, then it is even more important than usual that action is thought through. Time spent in reconnaissance is seldom wasted. Ill-considered action, which might reflect other approaches listed here, is never likely to work as well.

Considered and co-ordinated

Marketing activity must not be skimped. It must surely be done properly or not done at all. That does not mean that nothing other than elaborate and expensive action will prove useful. The reverse may well be true. But action must be considered. A great deal hangs on it, so it is surely worth some thought.

For most organisations the phrase 'marketing mix' is right. There is rarely one technique that works so well others are unnecessary. A mix is needed. Consideration, not least of what works best in the market, must lead to sensible decisions about which mix is the current 'best buy' for you. Then activity must be deployed *creatively* – ideas are important to marketing, which continues to be as much an art as a science. And the various activities must be well co-ordinated to get the most from them. It is this co-ordination that can help maximise the simplest mix – where one thing builds on another, adding power, and becoming a plan of action that is best for one simple reason – it does work and brings in the kind of business required, when it is wanted. Key approaches include making sure marketing activity is:

- reflecting a focus on customer attitudes, preferences and needs;
- embodying a considered approach (preferably linked to a plan);
- providing continuity – rather than acting in fits and starts;

- creative – ideas matter;
- well co-ordinated, so that different activities form a cohesive whole and act well together;
- regularly rethought, revised and updated.

To emphasise that marketing action must be got right, let me mention a saying attributed to Beverly Sills: 'There are no short cuts to any place worth going'. Good advice. And this timely book will surely help too. Its author is an experienced practitioner, we cross paths at CIM (Chartered Institute of Marketing) and I always find his perceptions and ideas useful. This book demonstrates his practical philosophy – whatever your marketing experience I believe you will find valuable ideas here that can help improve your marketing and profitability.

Patrick Forsyth is a consultant and trainer specialising in marketing and communications skills for professional service firms. He runs Touchstone Training & Consultancy and is a leading commentator on business matters with more than 50 successful business books published including: Marketing and Selling Professional Services *(Kogan Page),* The Management Speakers Handbook *(How to Books) and* Marketing: a guide to the fundamentals *(The Economist).*

Introduction

Welcome. I have good news for you. I believe that this book will provide you with a quickly accessible grand tour of most of what is important in marketing practice and its diverse constituent parts. It offers a rapidly digested insight into marketing's purpose and mechanisms, and it will give no small number of practical tips and examples to inspire you. Above all, you will find that this book is easy to understand, having been written with real people and plain language very much in mind.

If time is a pressing issue for you or if you have the attention span of a gnat, don't worry. This is a book that is designed for the pressured modern reader – it is meant to accommodate those whose preference is to dip in whenever the opportunity or the need presents. Alternatively, if your appetite is especially ravenous you can of course use it conventionally.

But why might you read this book at all? What do you want from marketing?

Assuming you exclude pure luck, business prosperity is a ship that must be steered by two masters. The first is known as the law of supply and demand. Take as an example the case of a roof thatcher. Many rural roofs are made of thatch but few experienced thatchers exist to keep them in good repair. The result is of course that those thatchers who are available are kept blissfully busy, set their own price and do not need to seek out employment opportunities. Nor do they need to promote their services or otherwise appreciate the deeper needs of would-be customers. However, for the remainder of commercial society the situation is notably less idyllic. Here, where supply comes closer to exceeding demand, there is a very real need to figure out how to get alongside new customers and attract both their attention and their patronage, while simultaneously outshining competitors – who rather irritatingly seem always to spoil our plans by introducing their own.

The second master required on the good ship prosperity is control. A continuously thriving organisation is much better prepared against the ups and downs of stormy weather. To remain busy the organisation must have a plentiful supply of customers and be in regular pursuit of yet more, which brings us back to marketing. For organisations that are not blessed with the good fortune of the thatcher, marketing is the mechanism which helps win customers and deprive competitors. It is also the mechanism that, if employed successfully, will enable control over where our organisation is headed. With marketing we have a greater chance not only to choose our destination but to arrive there; without it, who knows what might happen?

This book is written for a potentially broad readership:

Established businesses that want to know how to maintain or extend their customer base. **New businesses** that need to learn how to chart their course, pitch their offering, check their position and avoid dangers. **Public sector organisations** with private sector connections or a competitive role – those aiming to understand the commercial mindset. **Any organisational owner or manager** with a business development responsibility. **Non-marketing professionals** – regeneration officers, young enterprise teachers, charity promoters, etc. – wishing to gain marketing insight. **Marketing services buyers** wishing to understand the standards, aims or integrity of their sources. **Practising marketers** wishing to checklist their own actions or add supporting breadth to their proposals. **Business support advisors** operating beyond their specialities or wishing to extend their contribution. **Specialist providers** – designers, print providers, consultants, etc., wishing to affiliate with marketing processes and broaden their own horizons. **Anyone in business** who wants a quick access, single-source marketing industry 'bible' to keep at hand.

Marketing, though constantly evolving, is not a new professional discipline. It is also true to say that there are already a great many books and guides available on the subject. So why yet another – does this book contribute something especially significant? There are probably no radical new theories here though there are some new angles. The '4C foresight' view of an organisation's marketplace is my own development as is the 'lowerarchy of dependency' which cites that everything preceding the communication stages will be jeopardised if the communication itself is inadequate. I firmly believe that the role of communication in successful marketing is vastly underrated and all too often expedited by convenient yet unqualified souls. Consequently, you will find this book is deliberately slanted to antagonise that point. I have nothing against the legion of spotty nephews who supplement their allowance by knocking up a website or an ad – good luck to them – but I would sooner see more businesses take more interest and exhibit more professional pride in the way they convey themselves to their potential customers. You have but one chance to make a brilliant first impression, why waste it?

You will also come upon a few minor heresies. In a book that sets out to assist the acquisition of customers it might seem odd to you that I also propose that firing customers, should your organisation find itself serving those who fail to serve it, is the right thing to do. I also propose that business growth is not for all. Indeed some would be better served by resisting the temptation to grow if doing so is uncomfortable. The premise that underpins both these points is simply that your organisation's destination and the trappings of its journey should be pre-planned, not accidental. Getting there will be so much more enjoyable and productive if 'there' is correctly identified before departure.

Two features of this book probably are unique. Firstly, I know of no other that offers first-hand practical guidance on working with the various professional contributors that inhabit the marketing industry. The tools, tips and time-savers section provides a veritable Swiss Army knife of useful information. Secondly, in an attempt to keep this book's metaphorical feet on the ground and its language plain I have omitted much of the jargon and technical paraphernalia found elsewhere. A marketing book that fails to mention Vilfredo Pareto or Igor Ansoff by name, or to illustrate a BCG growth share matrix is, I submit, rare but probably all the more relevant to non-marketing practitioners as a result.

At the beginning of this introduction I mentioned good news – now for the bad. This book will not do your marketing for you. The sections it contains are not prescriptive. They represent the components – it is up to you to join them up and to act on the information they provide in whichever way best suits your circumstances. To help you, each section is concluded by a group of numbers, which represent related sections that you should also read. This step-by-step approach will help build your appreciation of the bigger marketing picture while keeping the effort required to absorb it contained in bite-sized chunks.

There are a few 'housekeeping' points to mention. Please accept the inadequate but universally understood word 'widget' as meaning your organisation's product or service offering. Please also accept use of the term 'your offering' to imply everything that you intend to sell to your customers. I am conscious of meandering back and forth between 'you' and 'your organisation' when I know that readers will be from organisations of all shapes and sizes, at all stages of development and growth – but it is cumbersome to keep saying as much. Please be assured that I mean to refer to all.

Some readers may notice (though hopefully not be irritated by) repetition of key principles. This is inevitable given the dip-in and dip-out nature of the book. It is best to repeat a worthwhile point in different places rather than risk not conveying it at all.

The majority of the content that follows is taken from my own workshop presentations. As a safeguard I have called upon others to check any aspects beyond my own focus. In addition to the contributions of those listed in the Acknowledgements I have cross-referenced material with responsible sources including the Knowledge Hub at the Chartered Institute of Marketing, the body of knowledge at The Institute of Business Consulting, Wikipedia and the business advice resource at Business Link, all of which I acknowledge with gratitude and have no hesitation in recommending to readers as sources for additional information. Every effort has been made to ensure that information provided in this book is up to date, accurate and appropriate. However, there is always a risk of oversight. The publishers and myself would welcome feedback from readers with observations to make about the present content or that which you feel should be included in subsequent editions.

Marketing is not magic – it is a management process. However much we might like the idea of wishing on a star the reality is that results come by shouldering the wheel. That said, the effect of those results can have a magical effect on the soul of any organisation whose fortunes are lifted to new heights of achievement by diligent application of marketing principles.

Onward and upwards.

Jeff Della Mura

Toto, I've a feeling we're not in Kansas anymore.

Dorothy – The Wizard of Oz

What to expect

Strong foundations are vital in supporting whatever ambitions come later – an explanation of the all-important first chapter.

If you're anything like me you'll be wanting to leap over the (often dull) introductory stuff and get quickly into the sections that seem more familiar, more interesting or less challenging. Please resist the temptation. Chapter 1 is important, very important. It will shape the way that the rest of this book works for you – and work for you it must, by providing the tools that will enable your personal capacity for progress. As far as I am aware, you will not come across the ten fundamentals of marketing elsewhere. They are my own interpretation of how modern marketing's set pieces can be organised. Be reassured that they are deliberately contrived to be easy to digest, simple to link and practical to act upon.

- By far the most efficient means of going nowhere is to do nothing. Apart from providing an explanation of what marketing can help you achieve, what it is and is not, you will find the thrust of this first section is that **only action creates action**. Success seldom arrives unprompted and without a degree of effort. To get somewhere you must do something. The good news is that you have already started.

- Developing your career or your business is clearly an important personal issue for you, otherwise we would not be having this conversation. Before you can set off effectively on the journey you need to know where and what you are right now. When you **know your business**, and know it well, you will have a greater understanding of how far both you and it can realistically expect to travel.

- For anyone with a demanding professional responsibility it is all too easy to become so consumed by day-to-day, even minute-by-minute, challenges that we mislay the plot. We sometimes see only as far as the boundary of our own organisation, often forgetting that beyond the walls there are other bees just like us in a megaplex of hives each pregnant with activity, opportunity and dangers. Looking and venturing beyond those walls is important – it's much easier to sell your honey if first you **know your market**.

- Good advice can come from surprising places. In *The Art of War*, written over 2,000 years ago, Chinese philosopher Sun Tzu warned, 'If you know yourself but not your enemy, for every victory gained you will also suffer a defeat'. The threat is clear and the suggestion is valid – **know thine enemy**. In competitive situations only one thing is certain: as long as there is a piece of the action to be had there will be somebody aiming to get more of it than you.

- Ignorance may well be bliss but the journey it inspires will not last long. In business there can be little doubt that **knowledge is power**. This section will explain how you can acquire the kind of knowledge that is useful – what it looks like and where it comes from.

- For some organisations merely having customers at all is a reason for contentment. They would doubtless argue that the role of the business is to serve the needs of its customers. True of course. But it is equally true that the role of the customers is to meet the needs of the business. The way to approach that state is by being selective – by **choosing the right customers**, even at the expense of the rest.

- As Lewis Carroll helpfully pointed out, if you don't know where you are going, any road will get you there. The problem is that you would not know if you had successfully arrived or unsuccessfully drifted way off course. The wise solution is to **pick your destination** in advance and prepare to recognise it (and yourself) when you arrive.

- Journeys undertaken without the benefit of a guide or a route map are devoid of landmarks and the potential for measurement or certainty, rather like attempting to prepare a meal without prior knowledge of its ingredients. **Planning is everything** if risk is to be reduced and progress is to be plotted with accuracy.

- Consider a baker, a bricklayer, a banker, a barrister and a bongo player. Imagine them naked and in a row. It is unlikely that you could identify their respective roles. But if you allow them their clothes and personal trappings, identifying what they are and how they differ becomes much easier. The same principle applies to the way your organisation is seen by potential customers. Until you **raise your flag** onlookers can't tell you apart or understand you. You risk being naked and, worse still, average.

- The last section in Chapter 1 reminds us that there is no advantage in being a best-kept secret. Your organisation must develop effective messages and **shout from the rooftops** so that would-be customers understand exactly what's on offer. Silence is not an option – we must communicate in an exciting, creative and purposeful way, using the correct techniques and language.

Whatever you think you can do or believe you can do, begin it.
Action has magic . . .

J W von Goethe

CHAPTER ONE

The ten fundamentals of marketing

In this chapter:

1. **Only action creates action** – what marketing is and why you need it
2. **Know your business** – what it is, how it is, where it is heading
3. **Know your market** – the four 'C' words that can determine your success
4. **Know thine enemy** – your customers will know them, shouldn't you?
5. **Knowledge is power** – making your market research work
6. **Choosing the right customers** – find the best ones, know what they want
7. **Pick your destination** – weigh the options and set your own agenda
8. **Planning for success** – forget the plans, but don't ignore the planning
9. **Raise your flag** – help customers to see you and understand you
10. **Shout from the rooftops** – the crucial role of marketing communications

1 Only action creates action

'Marketing activity helps you polish what you do best and identify what you should do more often. Important? Depends if you want to succeed.'

Wise organisations adopt management processes, which are measurable by their outcomes and repeatable by those who implement them. Such processes, including marketing, also give you control. Though it may soon change, the current Chartered Institute of Marketing definition describes the activity as '*The management process responsible for identifying, anticipating and satisfying customer requirements profitably*'. The keys are: process – manageable and repeatable; identifying – knowing not guessing; satisfying – not losing customers; and profitable – or you'll go to the wall. So, marketing is a systematic activity for keeping your customers and finding new ones. It can help keep you in business and help ensure that your business meets its objectives. With it, you get to control your destiny, without it your future is a matter of chance.

- The key aims of marketing are to retain **existing customers**, to recruit **new customers**, to increase the value of your sales and to maintain, or more ideally to grow, your share of the available market. Setting aside planning and distribution for the moment, the marketing process includes five actions: **knowledge** – understanding what the market wants; **alignment** – ensuring what you offer is what is wanted; **promotion** – announcing your offering; **transaction** – exchanging your goods or services for customer's money (usually); and finally, **repetition** – doing so again and again to build strength in your enterprise.

- **Marketing is not** advertising, though that is something which could be prompted by the marketing process. Nor is it sales or selling, but it does help you understand what to sell, to whom and at what cost. Selling is a separate activity that follows as a result of good marketing. **Marketing is** a tap best left dripping. It is most effective as a continuous process in which the relationship between an organisation and its customers – and of course its competitors too – is routinely examined and polished. It should not be treated like the family sledge and dragged out of the attic annually, or when the weather has already deteriorated.

Marketing is a tap best left dripping.

- Pleasing your customers requires that you understand, identify and emphasise the aspect of your service or product which customers value most. This must be based on their values – not your assumption of their values. Though this might sound simple it can often be difficult to pinpoint what makes customers value your widget more than someone else's.

- When looking at your market it is important to realise that you might not be able to satisfy the broad range of customers within it. To attempt to do so will mean that you must shape the appeal of your offering so widely that its strengths will be lost. The marketing process is geared towards **selecting the best customer targets** – even if this might mean dismissing others. If you aim at everyone you risk hitting no one.

If you aim at everyone you risk hitting no one.

- **Does marketing work for any organisation?** Yes it does. Wise organisations use marketing as a tool to facilitate their journey to the next stage of growth or consolidation. Marketing action will give those at the helm the opportunity to plan and control outcomes rather than leave matters in the fickle hands of fate. **Can anyone 'do' marketing?** Ultimately, the success of any undertaking will depend on the calibre and expertise of those involved. Be prepared to seek specialist support if doubts arise.

- Spike Milligan was helpful in explaining how not to do it. He said 'We haven't got a plan, so nothing can go wrong.' The only benefit of having no plan is that there are consequently no measures by which you might be judged. For tangible progress, something more substantial and methodical is required. As with any journey your chances of success will increase if you have a vision of your destination and a plan for getting there. Or, in more business-like terms, you should set your objectives, identify critical success factors and apply a strategy that will manage the process with least risk.

- **Your marketing strategy** should take realistic account of the conditions and circumstances surrounding it – or it just won't work. Insularity is a danger. If your organisation seeks to build a plan based around its own ego or habits the plan will probably fail or else be ineffective. The most successful and robust marketing strategies are

The most successful strategies are those focused on the needs of customers.

those focused outwardly on the market and specifically on the needs of customers.

- Any organisation, whether it's just you and a canary or you and several hundred other committed souls, can grow in three ways: **New customers**; **larger purchases** from known customers; and more frequent or **repeat purchases** from known customers. Marketing is the mechanism to stimulate and maintain all three routes.
- Some would-be entrepreneurs begin with a hot idea, and then seek a market for it. Sometimes the idea is interesting enough to appeal and a sustainable business is born. But more often than not, any business taking this approach will find itself in difficulty before too long. Good marketing practice seeks to lay reliable foundations that are underpinned by knowledge.
- The essence of successful marketing is understanding what your customers want – what they *really* want. Having understood what vital element captures your customer's interest your organisation must be flexible enough to deliver it – and flexible enough to change again and even again if that's what the market dictates. The swiftest route to obscurity is to ignore the market you serve or to assume you know what it wants without finding out for certain.

The swiftest route to obscurity is to ignore the market you serve.

Summary

Hope is not an adequate strategy. You cannot assume that those who sustain you (customers) will know you, find you, like you, prefer you or keep coming to you. Continuity and success tomorrow will depend on how effectively you take tangible action today. The appropriate action is marketing. It should be routine and central to the management of any organisation that aims to succeed. Marketing actions taken on the hoof or in an emergency do not work in the long term – it should be a continuous planned process. You may not be able to control your market but marketing will enable you to better control your relationship with it.

Also read sections: 2; 3; 4; 6; 8

2 Know your business

Nobody knows your business like you. But how much do you really know about where it is heading?

There will always be a sprinkling of successful businesses that rise to an enviable position on little more than good luck. However, if you plan to rely on this route the odds will not be in your favour. Successful businesses understand themselves and their trading environment. They use analytical tools to help them make decisions and manage risk. All wise organisations, regardless of their size, will benefit from understanding what it is that makes them tick. This point is fundamental if you intend to move forward and develop. And, of course, develop you will, because if you are any good at all you will understand that you could be even better. The fact is that until you know what and where you are, you cannot measurably move to somewhere else.

What is our purpose? . . . What is our vision? . . . What is our mission?

- Begin by asking the following questions: Who and what are we – **what is our purpose?** Where are we now and where do we want to be in the future – **what is our vision?** How will we get to where we want to be – **what is our mission?** PURPOSE is what you are, VISION is what you want to be, and MISSION is the practical action that will deliver the vision.

- Consider your **organisational objectives**. What do we do every day – what actions take place and why? Who are our customers? What influences us most – family, quality, profit, survival? How do we make our profit? Whether you or your organisation is motivated by wealth or by a desire to do good works you will need to profit before you can prosper and survive.

- As profit is ultimately what keeps you going it is vital to understand precisely what action generates it. If you can identify the action then you can amplify it and ensure that it does not become obscured or overwhelmed by other, less important distractions.

- Consider too your **organisational status**. What shape are we in right now – in control, stable or in crisis? What changes do we, or should we, have planned? Most importantly, what are our long-term goals? What resources do we have, or might we need to achieve those goals?

- No business audit would be complete without consideration of **the market**. You should first identify the market you serve, or intend to serve, and ask yourself how you will compete. A useful tool for revealing how an organisation fits into its market is the **SWOT analysis**. SWOT abbreviates strengths, weaknesses, opportunities and threats. **Strengths** – where and how are we stronger, smarter, better than those we compete against? **Weaknesses** – what do we need to improve, what do we lack? **Opportunities** – where are the market gaps that we can exploit, what is in our favour? **Threats** – what could topple us, where are we vulnerable?

- Strengths and weaknesses are internal matters that can be addressed from within the organisation. Opportunities and threats are subject to external influences and cannot be directly controlled. When compiling a SWOT analysis it is wise to set a limit for the response points against each heading. Five is usually ample.

- When analysing your **strengths and weaknesses** you can achieve additional clarity by measuring each of your **4 Ps (product, price, promotion, place) or 7 Ps (+people, process, perception)** individually against their own strength or weakness. Draw a vertical column and list the Ps on the left. Put a wider column to the right and enter your strength evaluations alongside each P. Repeat the process for weaknesses.

Product, Price, Promotion, Place, People, Process, Perception.

- As part of the SWOT analysis, specifically under the heading for **threats**, you can use a technique knows as **PEST analysis** to enhance your response. List the following words vertically on the left – **political, economic, social** (and environmental), **technological** – then use space on the right to analyse how external influences against each heading could have an adverse effect on your organisation. For example, against **political** you might consider if there are any current or forthcoming legal or cultural issues that could pose a threat. Similarly, against **economic** you could review how the financial climate could affect you.

- **Social and environmental** change are currently topical issues. Could they damage you and if so, what action could you take to minimise the effect? Lastly, **technological** threats. Change happens whether we like it or not. Though we cannot prevent change we can protect ourselves from it, or even exploit it, providing we look to see what's coming rather than permit ourselves to be caught off guard.

What are your unique features?

- Successful organisations plan and evaluate their businesses regularly, taking particular care to understand their competitors and their uniqueness. **What are your unique features?** The widgets might look the same but no two widget makers have the same characteristics. The sooner you can identify the magic ingredients in your business the sooner you can set about polishing and amplifying them.

Silence is not an option.

- **What do you do best?** Those organisations that understand exactly where they add most customer value and amplify their winning recipe are the ones that succeed. **How do customers view you?** Those within your organisation will know what its moral measures and values are. Those outside the organisation have no such insight – unless it is provided for them. So silence is not an option. **What can be improved?** In business things rarely stand still for long. Even if your prize-winning widget has a diamond in its navel, it might not retain its glitter forever. **Current and accurate knowledge** is essential.

Summary

Before you can set a course for where you'd like to be you must first reach an understanding of what and where you are now. Why does your business exist? What action creates profit? If you can first define your purpose and then your vision, achieving your mission will be much easier. Be sure you know your starting position and your intended destination. Knowing where your organisation is heading – preferably before the wagons are loaded and the journey begins – is fundamental for success. If you have no clue as to what your destination looks, feels and tastes like, how will you know if you have arrived there or if you missed?

Also read sections: 3; 6; 7; 13

3 Know your market

Before setting out your stall check that you have a good pitch and that you are in the right marketplace.

In an ideal world, all business organisations want to open their doors secure in the knowledge that their offering is wanted by those considered to be potential customers and that they are present in such numbers as to enhance the chances of success. Similarly, long established organisations will be concerned that no unwelcome usurpers arrive suddenly and undermine their stability. Any such ideal world is far removed from the competitive real world where nothing can be assumed or taken for granted. In these fast-moving, modern times very few organisations are immune from challenge or change. Knowledge is the key to survival and prosperity, knowledge of your customers and of your market. As Aristotle Onassis put it, '*The secret of business success is to know something that nobody else knows*'.

- Imagine a triangle with a letter 'C' in each corner. This is your marketplace. The 'C' in the lower right-hand corner stands for company – you. Your job is to build strength into your company, but to do that you need another 'C'. This one, at the top of the triangle, is 'C' for customers. Your company with customers on its doorstep – things look good . . . But wait, there's that other 'C' over on the left. That represents competitors – and they might want the customers that you want! Your market then is a dynamic balance between your **company**, your **customers** and your **competitors**.

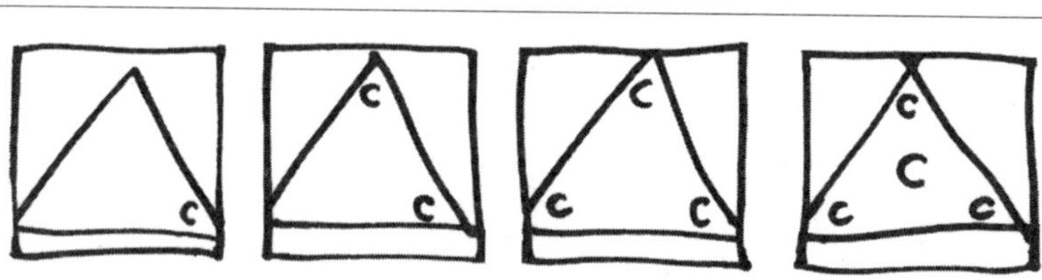

Market 4c foresight

© Jeff Della Mura 2008

- Your marketplace can become competitive but this doesn't necessarily spell disaster. The important thing is to appreciate that you are unlikely to have everything to yourself. Now add a fourth 'C' in the middle of your triangle. This one stands for **circumstances**. The one thing we all know about

The one thing we all know about circumstances is that they can change.

circumstances is that they can change. Again, this does not herald catastrophe providing you are prepared to meet change when it comes. Better still, according to marketer Andrew Chalk, develop market sensing skills to ensure you anticipate or even drive change.

- A market (also called a sector) is usually defined by industry type; for example, the automotive sector. The sector will include the specialised industry sub-divisions such as trucks, cars, vans and motorbikes. These sub-divisions are known as segments. Most organisations are too small to serve an entire sector. Instead, they usually focus on a specific segment. The benefit of concentrating on a segment is that buyers within it will share similar characteristics, making it easier to fine-tune your offering to fit the demand.

- So, **the whole market is a sector and the specialist sub-divisions are segments**. There's one more important feature that can be of considerable value – the niche. One American industrialist is rumoured to have said, 'There's riches in them nitches'. He was right about the principle, if not the grammar. A niche is a highly specialised fragment of a sector. Don't be misled by the word fragment – Rolls Royce motor cars are part of the luxury car niche within the cars segment of the automotive sector. Small niches often equate to big opportunities.

- Regardless of the type of market you serve, one golden rule will apply: No customers means no business. The more you can learn about **your customers** the closer you will be to winning and keeping them. Find out who they are, where they are, what they want, when and how they want it, what will they pay for it, what they think of you, what their buying preferences are, what you can do to win their attention and what might tempt them to buy elsewhere.

Find out who they are, where they are, what they want . . . and what they will pay.

- In learning more about your customers you will inevitably discover information about **your competitors**. Where possible, look at where and how they do business. Look at where they could be weaker or stronger then you. Seek and exploit gaps in the way they do things. Never forget that your customers probably know your competitors – you should too. It is imperative that you know more than they do!

Your customers probably know your competitors – you should too.

- The route taken by your product or service to your intended customers is called **the sales channel**. Consider the number of traditional retailers who have migrated from the high street to the internet in recent years and in so doing have completely shifted their sales channel. In some cases, where the retail outlet has been retained and supplemented by the online outlet, the business will have effectively opened a second sales channel. When planning your sales channel keep your focus on reaching the largest customer group, unless there's a good reason not to.

- If yours is a new venture you should **look carefully** at your market before leaping in. Consider the hapless soul who remortgaged his house and sold his wife and kids (apparently they were happier for it) to raise funds for a novel online venture. Not until almost £30,000 had been tipped into the bottomless pit of foolish endeavour did he discover that he was far from alone in his market. Around 200 other wannabees were all after the same throne. Ouch!

- Apparently, 80 per cent of the things we engage with daily did not exist 25 years ago. **Change** is a continuous, relentless process. (Wouldn't it be great to know how many of Detroit's wooden wagon makers watched the first vehicles drive off Henry Ford's production line and thought, 'It'll never last'.) In our digital age change can come fast. Markets, and the trends that govern them, alter continuously. The wise operator will deploy sensitive marketing antennae to stay one step ahead.

> **How many wooden wagon makers watched the first vehicles drive off Ford's production and thought 'It'll never last?'**

Summary

Look before you leap. Know your market and the components from which it is made. Remember the four Cs: company, customers, competitors and circumstances. Remember that circumstances cannot always be controlled. The whole market is a sector, which is split into segments, which contain niches. Most businesses serve either a sector or a niche. Understand where your customers are and what they want. Also study your competitors – what can you learn from them? Can technology help you streamline your sales channel? What changes could be on the horizon? Change can mean disaster for some but opportunity for others. Marketing can help you to exploit the opportunities.

Also read sections: 4; 5; 6; 8

4 Know thine enemy

No review of your market opportunity can be complete without considering your competitors – preferably before your customers get to know more than you do.

Competitors, rivals, the opposition or even the enemy, regardless of what you call them you should never forget that they can damage your business. Consider what would happen if your nearest competitor suddenly came up with a stunning widget that left your widget looking like the booby prize at a Losers' Ball. What if the enemy's widget proved to be technically superior, but cheaper than yours – where would that leave you? Fortunately, you are unlikely to be caught out like this if you study your competition. Business prosperity can depend on two things: your organisation's ability to continuously improve; and the enemy's ability to do so faster or better. There's real value to be had in understanding your competition – and you could be pleasantly surprised at how you compare.

- Ignore competitors or market trends and you risk being overtaken. Even the most loyal customers will at least be tempted to shift their allegiance for a better offer. Consequently, **gathering intelligence on the competition is** an **essential** component for your own success. Ideally, you should know who and where your main competitors are, what their business is, and how much they could affect your status quo. Don't overlook those who could become a problem in the future, especially new arrivals whose fresh approach and energy could challenge your position.

- Communications pioneer David Sarnoff commented that 'Competition brings out the best in products and the worst in people'. The more closely your products or services resemble those of your competition the more intense competitiveness will become. A more sensible philosophy is to strive to be different rather than similar. **Developing a tangible point of difference** will reduce the potential for debilitating conflict and help you to target defined customer groups to whom your offering can be tailored.

Competition brings out the best in products and the worst in people.

- You can legitimately learn a lot about the enemy and about your own business too by conducting a **comparative analysis**. Select key features such as product or brand awareness, price, service quality, product range or any other relevant attributes and then award yourself and your competitors comparative scores out of ten under each heading. The results should enable you to take appropriate action aimed at emphasising your strong points or strengthening weaker ones. Similarly, you could mount an opinion survey to **discover what customers think** or what they believe about you and your competition. You can apply the same approach to evaluating the effectiveness of your sales tools – literature, website, advertisements and so on.

- **Learn all you can** from the organisations at the head of your sector – those competitors you most admire and whose successes you would like to emulate. Study how and where they promote themselves. This could give valuable clues as to what type of media brings best results. That said, it could be unwise to advertise in exactly the same place, especially if the competitor has deeper pockets than you and can afford to create a bigger splash. If this is the case you might be better off taking a different media route.

Learn all you can from those . . . you most admire.

- The lengths to which some will go in pursuit of **competitor research** is a matter for personal morals. Consider for example the sales manager who faked a job application to gain a place on a two-week residential sales training course run by a major competitor. At the end of the course he resigned and went back to his own company taking a wealth of sales secrets with him.

He resigned and went back to his own company taking a wealth of sales secrets with him.

- Marketing professional Claire Lindsay recommends a spot of **mystery shopping**. See how quickly your competitors answer the phone or respond to requests for information. How do their products or services compare with yours? Do they brag about imminent technical advances? Do their delivery times eclipse yours? How does the customer service experience compare?

- Keep a close watch on **competitor websites**, the trade press and recruitment pages. These sources will often reveal what competitor firms say about themselves and their future plans. If they are recruiting or looking for new premises it could mean that something big is in the wind. You may not be able to stop it but you could arrange a trade PR event of your own that could perhaps dilute its impact.

- Gathering useful information on your competitors is a legitimate component of marketing, but care needs to be taken. Talking to your rival's disgruntled ex-staff might lead to some very interesting discoveries, but be aware that you could find yourself on the wrong side of the law for inducing a breach of confidence if the former staff member was bound by a contractual confidentiality clause.

Gathering useful information on your competitors is a legitimate component of marketing.

- Similarly, where confidential **product development** information is concerned there is a fine legal line between picking up useful information on the grapevine and misappropriation of information by improper means. Generally speaking, the clue, assuming you'd sooner stay out of gaol, is this: if information can be readily found in the public domain it cannot be classed as a trade secret. Before you attempt to organise phone taps or hire computer hackers please consider this: competitive research and gathering **competitive intelligence** are legal activities; corporate espionage is not.
- If you want a highly detailed view of your competition and of the market in general you can appoint a Competitive Intelligence Agency. These folks know the ropes and, importantly, they know where the legal lines are drawn.

Summary

Very few organisations can bask in the luxury of having nothing to beat or to measure themselves against. Fewer still have nothing to fear from a market that could suddenly change. Keeping a watchful eye on competitors is a necessity if you want to avoid being outmanoeuvred or outmoded. This shouldn't be seen as a chore but rather as a way of strengthening your chances of success. If you're in any way passionate about the business you're in and the market that you serve (and if you're not, maybe it's time for a rethink), finding out what's going on around you should be a natural, seamless habit.

Also read sections: 5; 11; 14

5 Knowledge is power

'Guessing is free, but also unreliable. If you want to know how much you don't know, market research is the way to find out.'

The purpose of market research is to gain information that will help reduce risk and enable a greater understanding of the market you are in, or thinking of being in. It should be seen as intelligence from which future strategies can be shaped. Research can help establish if you are selling the right things, if you are doing so in the right way and if your marketing plans and efforts are appropriate. It can also provide a competitive advantage – or even prevent you becoming a victim of somebody else's. Market research is win-win. Discover bad news then you can plan afresh to avoid problems. Discover encouraging news, then you can move forward with added confidence. The more you know, the further you'll go.

Research should be RELEVANT, RELIABLE and RESOUNDING.

- Research that is random or unsubstantiated is of little value. If it is to be worthwhile, research should lead to action – as a means to an end, not the end in itself. The golden maxim is that market research should be RELEVANT, RELIABLE and RESOUNDING. In his defining book, *Marketing Research: An Integrated Approach*, Professor Alan Wilson emphasises that research and its interpretation are key elements of marketing – not merely a side issue for statisticians.

- Research falls into one of two categories: primary research – the collection of new information by, for example, customer interviews or test marketing; and secondary research – the use of information already gathered, such as government statistics or general trends analysis. Professionals do the secondary research first.

- Research provides two types of information – **qualitative**, which is oriented towards softer issues such as impressions or opinions, and **quantitative**, which is focused on numbers and accountable data. The nature of your objective should dictate the option or the mixture you adopt. If you want opinions it is best to ask **open questions** that enable the contributor to respond in their own words. However, this can be difficult to correlate and time-consuming to conduct. The process can be speeded up by using **closed questions** or 'yes, no, maybe' options, but these will require the questions to be very precisely posed.

- Common examples of market research include **competitive analysis** and **performance comparison**, whereby an organisation can compare itself against competitors using criteria such as market targets and share pricing, brand recognition, perceived quality, unit costs and so on. Alternatively, **consumer research** would seek to establish customer opinions, needs or preferences, satisfaction, future trends and so forth. Another variant is **sector research**, in which the size of a known market segment is analysed to provide a forecast of future sales potential.

- **Product development research** – assessing the potential for incrementally improved products, where the subject is already recognised and can be compared easily with an outmoded version – is relatively reliable. However, truly innovative products or ideas that have not been seen before are difficult to research objectively because there is nothing to compare them with. Examples of innovative successes that initially failed to impress in their embryonic stage include Coca-Cola, the telephone, the automobile, Elvis Presley, personal mobile music and the cyclonic vacuum cleaner.

> **Examples that failed to impress include the telephone, the automobile, Elvis Presley and the cyclonic vacuum cleaner.**

- When using consumer research techniques such as **focus groups**, where a group of potential consumers is brought together and asked probing questions, care must be taken to ensure that the guest 'consumers' are genuinely representative of the actual or desired customer type. Friends and allies seldom provide objective feedback.

> **Friends and allies seldom provide objective feedback.**

- There are two **crucial decisions** that must be made accurately before any form of market research proceeds. Firstly, define exactly what you need to learn and secondly, define the source that will have the information. Once you know what you are looking for it becomes much easier to establish what type of **research technique** you should use. The approach can be: simple, informal **verbal questions**; or formal, a **written survey**; or complex, **whole-market analysis** or technically sophisticated **data mining**.

- There is no matrix for selecting the most apt **research method**. The right method is the one that best suits your circumstances. However, there are three questions that will help steer your choice. How much time or money do you have? How accurate do you need to be? And, where are the potential respondents?

> **When working with an alphabetical sample group start at Z and work backwards.**

- When working with an alphabetical sample group start at Z and work backwards. These targets will be less resistant to questions, having been interviewed less often. **Never** put highly personal, intrusive or uncomfortable questions near the beginning of a survey or questionnaire. Being asked how much you earn by a complete stranger, or worse still, by an online survey, can switch respondents off. If you want to **switch respondents on** and open their natural defence shield, ask two neutral questions that generate a comfortable 'yes' response before you begin your real questions.
- If you are intending to present your research findings to a higher authority always name influential sources if confidentiality permits. It will also add weight to the credibility of your findings if you highlight the methods used to obtain information and mention any controls used to screen inappropriate conclusions. **Never** publish information generated by or belonging to others without their permission. If in doubt, seek legal advice. Ensure that the way information is obtained does not discredit the results achieved. If you are old enough, you will remember Watergate. If you're not, you could look it up – it will be good research practice.

Summary

Market research provides a torch to light the way ahead and offers the opportunity to gain an informed understanding of your business prospects. It aims to replace guesswork with knowledge and it can be employed at any stage of a business or product cycle – unless of course you are researching the pros and cons of a new business step, in which case you should research before rather than after the event. The quality of the answers you get will be dictated by the care you take in pinpointing what needs to be known. Always analyse realistically – look for the actual answer not the one you were hoping for. Check your obligations under the Data Protection Act and the Market Research Society Code of Conduct.

Also read sections: 12; 13; 41

6 Choosing the right customers

'There's no need to waste your energy shooting in the dark when you could be targeting the very customers that can move you forward.'

Modern markets can be confused, competitive and awkward to serve, which means they are also awkward to market to. The situation becomes easier if we take a more selective approach. Rather than aiming to attract just ANY customers, wise organisations focus their efforts on the RIGHT customers. They will be accessible – we must be able to reach them; they will be profitable – or else there's no point; they will be scaleable – present in beneficial numbers; they will be easy to serve – having similar characteristics; and they will be so well suited to our offering that competitors will be disadvantaged. Dr Brian Smith, author of *Creating Marketing Insight* adds this point, '*Good marketing strategies shape offers aimed at where the market is going, not where it is or was*'.

Only option one provides an opportunity to build a sustainable position.

- Commercial organisations have three possible routes towards a competitive advantage. **Option one**: provide high quality at a high price to those customers willing to pay a premium. **Option two**: reduce the cost (and inevitably the standard) and aim for customers who prefer cheaper deals. **Option three**: hedge your bets and mix options one and two. Which of these is most likely to provide a sustainable competitive position? Let's look at them again in reverse order. Option three will make it difficult for you to stand out or to develop a single-minded brand personality. If you adopt option two you will continuously find yourself fending off competitors willing to match or even beat your price. Worse still, you will be courting the most disloyal customer group of all – those who are driven (anywhere) by price alone. Only option one provides an opportunity to build a sustainable, profitable business position.

- The way forward is to **segment the market** and locate the customer group or groups (segments) that most closely match your preferred business model. Be mindful that you cannot create a segment of like-minded customers – they exist already as part of the natural process that forms markets. However, what you can do is to find the right segment for you and align yourself with it.

> **Customers in any given segment act the same way.**

- Put simply, a segment is a division of the market in which the customers share common characteristics and motivations. For example, an automotive manufacturer might only be interested in customers who want family cars. Because these customers will think along similar lines it makes the job of marketing to them much easier. If the customers in any given segment act the same way (and if they don't you may not have a true segment) it can be assumed that they will also respond in the same way when approached with a marketing proposition.
- There are other benefits of segmentation. Finer targeting helps save on promotional costs. The promotional process is simplified by having a closer understanding of those it is aimed at – and if it becomes simple it will probably also be more efficient. In addition, because businesses select segments to which their offering is well suited, it follows that the business is automatically able to work to its strengths, thereby reducing the potential for head-on competitiveness.
- By their very nature, market segments contain groups of customers whose behaviour or motivation is in some way unique or individually characteristic to such an extent that the differences between any two segments are clear. In other words, no two segments can be the same. Therefore, a marketing solution that applies successfully to one segment is unlikely to work for others, which is why businesses cannot meet the needs of multiple true segments simultaneously.
- When seeking an appropriate segment many organisations start by looking at their own products and services. These are relevant but they do not represent the whole story. Truly effective segmentation is about looking at the customers that most closely meet the needs of the organisation, then adjusting what the organisation does until the fit becomes snug. Marketers call this process '**alignment**'.

> **In aligning their offering organisations should be prepared to re-shape themselves.**

- In aligning they're offering to match the requirements of the chosen segments, organisations should be prepared to re-shape themselves and, if necessary, to discard unhelpful traits that might otherwise prevent their offering becoming fully attuned to the segment.
- To find advantageous segments organisations usually look for common behaviour or attributes such as lifestyle, age, gender or

professional interests and so on. Actual, proven personal attitudes are stronger and therefore far more reliable as indicators of real segments than, for example, geographic location, which might put a person in a particular place but it will not denote whether that person is, say, a vegetarian or fond of fine wine. Those who comprise the segment must be seen in the way they see themselves and not necessarily as demographic data would define them. The key here is good research and creative insight.

- Here's an example of segmentation at work. There are two Indian restaurants in my home town. Unfortunately, they are opposite each other on the same street. Inevitably, they both compete for the same market – that is everyone who lives locally and enjoys Indian food. Rather than compete head-on they have each found their own market segment. One has pitched their offering up-market. They sell cuisine rather than food and have created a high quality, stylish ambience. The other has introduced buffet-style menu packages and Karaoke, which in turn has encouraged party bookings. Both restaurants can coexist profitably and focus their energies on developing their customer segments rather than in competing against each other.

> **Rather than compete head-on they have found their own segment.**

Summary

IDENTIFY the customers that are most profitable; PROFILE them to understand their motivations and characteristics; SEGMENT the wider market and look for groups of customers who share the characteristics of the profiled sample; TARGET those groups with your marketing; ALIGN your offering to fit the target group's needs. This process will get you closer to your customers, reduce promotional waste and reduce the potential for head-on competitive action. It should also allow you to further develop your strong points. On the downside, each segment you cultivate will require a separate marketing mix. Don't overlook your existing customers.

Also read sections 3; 7; 11; 18

7 Pick your destination

Weigh the options and set your own agenda for building your organisation and its place in customers' minds.

The market that your organisation serves and the prevailing circumstances surrounding it will play an influential role in your destiny. Market features tend to define themselves, suggesting vigilance and caution. However, wise organisations will still lay positive plans to define and control the way they fit into their market and the way they are perceived by their customers. Wise organisations will seek to be different and to provide themselves with competitive advantages – they will embrace the various options for differentiation and they will sculpt their own style. There is little benefit in being one of many but much to be said for being unique. Thereafter, continuous development is compulsory if you want to keep up, but market growth remains optional. Providence aside, the course you follow is up to you.

Head-to-head, attritional competition is best avoided.

- **Differentiation** equates to a competitive advantage. If your organisation settles for being exactly the same as its competitors it will be exposed to two disadvantages. Firstly, direct competition, which is both draining and expensive. Secondly, your customers will find it difficult to identify and select you in preference to others. Head-to-head, attritional competition is best avoided, the most straightforward way of doing so is by being different – differentiation.

Add value rather than reduce price.

- There are four ways in which an organisationn can set itself apart. The first is **Price Differentiation**, which requires a considered approach. The most obvious strategy might be to attempt to outstrip your competitors by being less expensive. However, this will be difficult to maintain and will ultimately result in less revenue and diminished quality, which will in turn alienate customers. The ideal position is to be more expensive than your competitors, but justifiably so on account of the higher value (not price but value) of your offering. Add value rather than reduce price.

- **Focus Differentiation** helps to define how your organisation aims to specialise within its field. Are you, within an industry of widget makers, known particularly for being easy to deal with, or offering a shorter response time, or longer opening times? Do you place a particular emphasis on providing a wider selection of related products to go with your widgets, or is your preference to exclude peripherals and focus totally on a single high quality output?

- **Product or Service Differentiation** is one fairly obvious way for an organisation to become a favoured customer choice. But remember that the market you are in will influence the extent to which your organisation can distinguish itself. All organisations would like to be leaders or innovators but in some markets this is unrealistic. However, you can still set your offering apart by looking closely at notable ways of customising or presenting it, or of adding benefits to enhance its impact on customers.
- **Customer Service Differentiation** is closely linked to how well your organisation knows and understands its customers and their deep-rooted needs. Consider all the things that help generate customer comfort – guaranteed service times, after sales support, a helpline, free delivery, exemplary service levels, no-quibble exchange policy. Coincidentally, these are also the kind of things that customers will talk about, so enhancing your reputation becomes part of the gain too.
- Collectively, these aspects of differentiation will influence the way your organisation is perceived by its intended customers. The aim is to present a unique system of attributes that are automatically linked in the customer's mind to become the factors that govern their preferences and position your organisation as the first choice.
- **Distribution** – the means by which your customers might meet your offering – can also provide an opportunity for differentiation. Consider how some traditional retail outlets have enabled online purchasing and home delivery, thus setting themselves apart and gaining a competitive advantage. How do your customers meet with your offering? Are there notable weaknesses or strengths in your distribution method? Could emerging technology enable you to introduce an innovative point of difference?
- **Unique Selling Proposition** (USP) is the marketing term used to describe what it is that makes your organisation special or what helps it stand out in a crowded marketplace. Usually, a USP is related to being better (quality, value, service) than your competitors or else closer (in-touch,

Your USP is what sets you apart.

attentive) to your customers. Either way, the USP is a summary of how you or your organisation can be differentiated. What is your USP?

- Deciding what your organisation is – or what market circumstances permit it to be – leads inevitably to consideration about where it is heading. For most, standing still is not an option. Continuous development is usually necessary to ensure future viability. The matter of organisational development is inextricably linked with the option of extending market opportunities.

- Market growth can be achieved in four ways. In ascending order of associated risk these are firstly, by **Market Penetration**, normally by stimulating additional buyer interest. Secondly, **Market Development**, which aims to extend the sale of existing products into new or parallel markets. The third option is **Product Development** in which entirely new or complementary products are introduced into your existing market. Lastly – and carrying most risk of all – **Diversification**, which is concerned with developing new products for new, untried markets.

Growth can be achieved in four ways.

Summary

Differentiation means separating yourself from 'me-too' competitors. Being different reduces the expense and effect of head-to-head direct competition. Being different gives customers a means of identifying you and choosing you out of preference. Key differentiators are price – and added value; focus – and specialised traits; product or service – customised to satisfy customer needs; and finally, customer service – creating a comfort level. Collectively, these differentiators act to form your unique selling proposition and to position your offering in customers' minds. Market growth can occur by four optional routes, each with varying levels of risk. Market growth is dependent on organisational ambition. Continuous organisational development is a must.

Also read sections: 3; 9; 11; 21

8 Planning for success

Dwight Eisenhower knew the value of putting quality effort in to get quality results out. He said – **"Plans are nothing, planning is everything".**

Marketing ambitions require a marketing plan. More instinctive actions may work for a while but, sooner or later, as the need for sustainable growth kicks in, luck and intuition can run out. The fact is that organisations wanting to progress need to plan. They will move further, faster, with fewer mistakes than those who do not. Furthermore, a plan that exists only in your head is not a plan at all but a loose collection of ideas and hopes. The only plan that will work effectively is one that is objective, systematic, measurable – and written down. Your marketing plan will act as a route map and help you to avoid obstacles or nasty surprises. The good news is that it need not be complicated to achieve.

- **The ultimate aim of marketing**, and indirectly, of your marketing plan, is to ensure your organisation remains viable and profitable. The plan itself need not be lengthy to be worthwhile. Five or six pages are enough. The most important aspect of the plan is the process you go through to form it. What goes in will dictate what comes out.

The most important aspect of the plan is the process you go through to form it.

- In compiling **your marketing plan** you will need to consider pertinent background information before forming a strategy. To produce your plan, list the following component headings and work your way through them using this section and everything you read in Chapter 1 as your guide: the organisation, current situation and future objectives; the market you serve; the customer segment you target; market overview; organisational review and SWOT; marketing objectives; marketing strategy; the budget; people; and action checklist.

- **Define your organisation.** The first step is to write a short executive summary that sets the scene. Summarise your current situation – what's going on – where are you now? What are your short- and longer-term ambitions? This should be followed by a brief declaration of where you want to be or the position you want to move towards. This is your **business or organisational objective** and the role of marketing is to support it.

- **Define the market you are in.** You should do this from your customers' viewpoint. Most organisations answer this question by stating what they do, using their product or service definition. So a restaurateur might claim to be in the catering market. However, customers at the restaurant might not be going there for the catering but for a leisure experience so it's debatable whether the business serves the catering market or the leisure market. The market served by an organisation should be defined by what the customers in it think they are buying, not what the organisation thinks it is selling.

> **The market should be defined by what the customers are buying, not what the organisation is selling.**

- **Define the segment you serve.** A segment is the slice of the market that is most promising for your situation or ambitions. It is classified by the shared characteristics of the customers within it. Your aim should be to match your own strengths to their preferences. Wise organisations put the needs of the market first. **Consider the market in general**. Look at what your competitors are doing and, where possible, aim to avoid them by being different. Is the market growing or shrinking? Are there any significant changes on the horizon?

- **Conduct an organisational review** including a **SWOT analysis** (Strengths, Weaknesses, Opportunities and Threats) to establish how you fit into your market. What you learn at this stage will help confirm if your outline marketing objectives are appropriate and realistic. Incidentally, marketing objectives need not be complex. They could include simple aims such as retaining current customers or achieving a 10 per cent increase in turnover. The IMPORTANT thing is that they should be specific and measurable.

> **Marketing objectives need not be complex but they should be specific.**

- **To summarise**, you will have established your current situation and your long-term aims, you will have identified the market you serve and, more specifically, which segment of that market you are targeting. And you have conducted a SWOT analysis. By weighing up the information you have gathered, you can now confirm your **marketing objectives** (the specific goals and milestones) and form your **marketing strategy** (the methods that will meet your goals).

- Before the plan can be finalised two elements must be confirmed. First, **the budget**, which should ideally fit the cost of the exercise rather than dictate the extent of it. You should know how much the marketing exercise will cost to implement and how your organisation will benefit. Wise organisations prepare three forecasts – optimistic, realistic and pessimistic. Established organisations can use past experience as a base for forecasts but new businesses or new products will inevitably require some cautious assumptions. Second, **the people**. Those who will implement or be affected by the plan must 'buy' into it fully. If not, the plan could fail to be effective.

- **Action checklist.** It is vital that your marketing plan links with a plan of action that will move it from theory to reality. This should include a summary of what is going to happen and when; who is going to manage each of the component parts; what tools or external services may be required; relevant dates and time-paths and built-in **monitoring points**.

It is vital that your marketing plan links with a plan of action that will move it forward.

- **Test your plan** if possible, perhaps on a sample group, before deploying it fully. **Monitor** progress and make adjustments as required. **Measure** and record critical success factors before the plan goes live and as it progresses so that you can see and gauge change. Outcomes should be quantifiable.

Summary

The marketing plan should support the aims of the business plan. Marketing planning will help ensure that any actions you take are properly thought through. Key features are that the plan should be written and succinct. It should be factual – realistic and to the point, starting with a short executive summary and ending with an action checklist. It should set out the steps for progress and be costed and timed. Importantly, it should be specific and its results measurable. Build-in regular monitoring points and make step-by-step adjustments as necessary. Include ethical and sustainability considerations where apt.

Also read sections: 2; 3; 6; 7; 13

9 Raise your flag

Before they can buy from you, your customers need to see you, understand you, trust you and even appreciate you.

Yours might be the most wonderful widget in an entire universe of widgets but unless those you would have as customers know about it your ambitions could fail. Your organisation might provide the warmest of welcomes but if those you would greet can't find you, your warmth will be wasted. Making and keeping friends commercially is not hugely different from doing so socially. First you have to meet, then make an effort to understand each other. Providing there is willingness on both sides the relationship will grow. This is a simplification of course but the principles for business are sound. All organisations must strive to make or attract new contacts and, having done so, must reveal their personality to tempt and keep customer interest.

Stop thinking of commodities, start thinking of 'benefits'.

- Understand your customers. Start by looking at what you achieve for them. Not what you sell to them but what the sale does – its effect on their lives. Stop thinking of commodities, start thinking of 'benefits'. For example, a clothier might well sell tailoring skills but the result is that the customer feels smarter, attractive and more confident. So the organisation is not in the clothing business but in the personal confidence business. Once you know what your customers really want you will understand what business you are really in. When you understand that, explaining your offering will be easier. **What business are you really in?**

- When you understand the true role of your organisation you can begin forming the messages that will help others to understand and evaluate you. Consider the benefits you provide and, importantly, identify the special aspect or features that set your organisation apart from others. Marketers call this the unique selling proposition or USP. Your USP can be based on the way your organisation goes about things or the experience it provides for customers. Barry Ardley, Senior Lecturer in Marketing at Lincoln University, suggests you go one step further than competitors in finding extra value propositions that will help you stand out. **What do you do that is unique?**

- It is important that those within an organisation are aware of its USP. It will help if you develop an 'elevator speech' and encourage your team to learn it. Typically this can be seen as a response to the hypothetical question 'So, what do you do?' or 'What business are you in?' The best replies don't merely explain what you do, they also inject a positive note and prompt a further question. For example, rather than say, 'We make blue widgets,' you could try, 'Well, you know all those people out there who rely on blue widgets? We keep them happy in a really special way . . .' **What is your elevator speech?**

- There are two useful ways to help customers understand you. First, you can build a good reputation (referrals are around four times more effective than advertising). Second, you can improve the effectiveness of your customer-facing messages by using the terms customers would use. Check regularly how they describe your products or services and compare their terminology against yours. **How do customers describe you?**

Referrals are around four times more effective than advertising.

- Being a best-kept secret is not an option. Organisations must be apparent if they are to be noticed and patronised. Check your visibility against the following points: Is your name memorable and easy to use? Is it always presented in the same way? If your products or services are sub-branded do they share a common unifying feature? Your premises, your signage, your advertising style, staff behaviour, slogan, website, stationery, packaging, etc., should all contribute to the image and brand message that will help customers identify you. **How visible is your organisation?**

- Customers will only recognise you if it interests them or is easy for them to do so. That could depend on how effective your USP is or how much you help them by demonstrating consistent behaviour, values, appearance and performance. These are the elements that are rooted in your brand identity. For people to know you, then (critically) to trust you, consistency is key. **How recognisable is your organisation?**

How recognisable is your organisation?

- Perception IS reality. Your organisation can create a magnetic image that will favourably influence customers simply by sowing seeds of belief. The options for success will involve being seen as better than the competition or, alternatively, being closer to the customer. However, there needs to be substance too. No organisation can exist on a contrived reputation for long. Wise organisations aim to exceed customer expectations. **Does your organisation exceed expectations?**

- As Robert Burns, Scotland's favourite observer of human traits observed, the way we see ourselves is one thing but the way others see us is what really matters.

  Wise organisations check frequently that self-opinion matches customer opinion.

  Oh wad some power the giftie gie us, to see oursels as others see us!

  Wise organisations check frequently that self-opinion matches customer opinion and the first step to perfection is to identify and rectify imperfections. There is nothing wrong with not having everything exactly right, but there is plenty wrong with leaving it that way. **What do customers think of you?**

- Perhaps the most difficult and elusive prize of all is winning the affection of customers. Not their patronage but their genuine affection – the emotional bond that will prompt them to automatically reject the notion of going elsewhere (and to recommend that their friends and connections do likewise). Customer loyalty can be won. It should most certainly be sought because it will reduce the effort you would otherwise have to put into marketing. **Do your customers value you?**

Summary

Success requires that we understand our customers and make it **easy** for them to understand us. Organisations must be **easy** to find, they must also be **easy** to recognise and **easy** to separate from competitors by their values, behaviour, icons and special features. With diligence, reputations can be built that will render it **easy** to form invaluable bonds of trust. No customer returns willingly to the scene of a struggle – organisations must be **easy** to buy from and **easy** to get along with. If we are to find a place in our customers' minds and possibly their hearts too we should not overlook the obvious – we must be **easy** to like.

Also read sections: 7; 11; 17; 21; 38

10 Shout from the rooftops

'The role of marketing communications is crucial in conveying news of your product or service and the message behind your brand.'

The cumbersome epithet 'marketing communications' refers to the way an organisation speaks to its customers or potential customers. The methods or channels used to deliver the message can be diverse – websites, brochures, radio ads and so on. However, the role of communication in the greater marketing process is more specific, namely to distinguish the organisation and carry news of its offering to the target audience, usually with the intention of persuading them to engage and invariably in such a way as to lead to a sale. Although marketing communications, or 'marcoms' as the activity is sometimes more conveniently called, is the term most often associated with advertising or promotional materials, there is also a broader application, which can include almost anything else that usefully extends the influencing process.

Action to inform and influence your target market.

- Unless you are a rare exception, the chances are that you take some kind of action to inform and influence your target market – your customers or intended customers. Specifically, the action will be to proactively promote your offering by communicating what it is, and why it is meaningful to your targets. Paul Weeks, Senior Lecturer at Anglia Ruskin University explains: '*New customers will need to know who, what and where you are before they can buy from you. They will also need to recognise and understand you and be able to evaluate what benefits you provide. Existing customers will be reassured that you are still active and will be interested in new information.*'

- Understanding of both the greater marketplace and of the selected target segment (or segments) should underpin marcoms planning. Reliable market knowledge will increase the likelihood of effective communication, which in turn will enhance your chances of success. Think of it as a building – thorough surveying provides appropriate foundations that enable a better wall.

- Marketing communications should help you achieve most, if not all, of six key objectives. These are: to **influence**; to **inform**; to **promote**; to **remind**; to **differentiate**, and to **persuade**. Your communications strategy should also fulfil your **organisational objectives** – the big picture stuff behind everything you do; your **brand objectives** – the values that shape the business; and your **marketing objectives** – the purpose of the communication.

To influence, inform, promote, remind, differentiate and persuade.

- Marketing communications serve your marketing strategy. You should know in advance who will be reached, how they might respond and how you will benefit as a result. Ideally, there should be a direct relationship between what you expect from your marketing communications and the extent of the budget at your disposal. In other words the wallet should match the ambition.

- Budget setting in larger organisations typically results in a tug-of-war between the marketing department and the Finance Director. Inevitably, this leads either to a disappointment for somebody or a compromise for everybody. In smaller businesses the most common discovery is that there is no formal marketing budget at all. **Wrong!** Promoting the business is part of the management function and should be seen as a running cost in the same way as salaries, rent or utility bills.

- As with other management processes, performance measurement of the marketing function is a sensible habit. The success of your marketing communications should be evidenced by how effective they are compared with what they cost to deploy and what benefits they bring to the business. Remember that your marketing communications do not always need to be focused directly on driving sales, but can also apply to any item or action that promotes a greater understanding of the business or of the brand. Every email, phone call, letterhead, or door sign also provides an opportunity to influence.

- Though most marketing-oriented communication is likely to be directed outwards from the organisation towards its customers, the opportunity to influence inwardly should not be overlooked. Keeping internal stakeholders informed will help to form a uniform understanding of what the organisation does, what its key messages are and what it does to pay its way.

- A common challenge faced by marketers and communicators is the absolute necessity of cutting through the huge amount of competitor 'noise' that screens intended recipients. The vital ingredients in overcoming this snag are impact and

Not as a result of making a louder noise but by making a smarter noise.

difference – not necessarily as a result of making a louder noise but **preferably by making a smarter noise** that penetrates under the target's radar. Therefore, you should treat the temptation of DIY solutions with care. 'Cheap' will please the finance department but it may not compete with the enemy sufficiently to deliver results for the sales department.

- The methods or channels through which marketing communications can be routed are varied and should be selected for their ability to deliver the message most efficiently to the largest possible appropriate audience. In reality, this ambition is sometimes subverted by what is most affordable or what has become habitual. The options available include advertising, public relations, sales promotion, direct marketing, personal selling and more.
- Regardless of which channel of communication is selected to deliver it, the message itself should be built around the needs, language, preferences and expectations of the receiver – not the agenda, jargon, ambitions or baggage of the sender. Consistency should touch everything. If all that your organisation produces bears a consistent look and feel it will convey a sense of order and unity, which in turn will suggest that the organisation itself is well ordered and performs in a unified way. This sends a strong signal about calibre.

The message should be built around the language and expectations of the receiver – not the sender.

Summary

To succeed in business you need to sell. You will need to first explain your offering. This means that some form of marketing communication is required – effective methods and messages that will cut through barriers. Your aim will be to send the right message, to the right targets, using the right method and, all being well!, achieving the right results. No organisational communication should take place without purpose or without some means of evaluating its effectiveness. No communication should occur that fails to enhance or credit the organisation that produced it. Finally, no communication should be untruthful, misleading, offensive, criminal or otherwise in breach of law.

Also read sections: 3; 11; 18; 20; 21; 28

CHAPTER TWO

The stepping-stones to success

In this chapter:

11. **Building a brilliant brand** – creating great value from great values
12. **Measuring performance** – what works, what doesn't and what next?
13. **Think strategically** – know why you're doing it, before you do it
14. **Sales and selling** – the cold facts about warming up sales

11 Building a brilliant brand

Build customer loyalty with credible trust and warm reassurance, not bribes and offers. It's about creating great value from great values.

The great attraction of brilliant brands is that they tend to enjoy ready popularity and higher comparative profits. Brand building, therefore, is a sensible marketing action. Don't make the mistake of thinking that this is just a costly exercise for huge corporates because it isn't. Every business is capable of developing customer loyalty based on the intangible relationship that exists between the organisation and its customers – you probably have a preference for a particular grocery store even though there are others in town. Brilliant brands sell more easily, more consistently and more profitably. For these reasons alone brands are useful, but there's more. Well-nurtured brands can also become an investment, which can be trademark protected – if it's protectable, then it's ownable – and potentially valuable.

- The brand is not the logo, which serves a different purpose. The brand summarises the way an organisation is perceived by its customers or potential customers. It does not exist physically but as an impression in people's minds. As an emotional belief nurtured in customers' affections, brands can become very powerful in steering purchase decisions. Lincoln University's Barry Ardley reminds us that successful brands are memorable, meaningful, likeable, transferable, adaptable and protectable.

- Consumers do not merely buy products or services, they prefer to buy into a closer bond with a familiar and trusted friend. **A successful brand builds a relationship** with its customers that goes beyond simply exchanging a commodity for money. This relationship can turn a dithering purchase decision into an automatic 'no brainer' and can cement customer loyalty, which explains why powerful brands are such favourites with marketers.

> **Consumers prefer to buy into a closer bond with a familiar and trusted friend.**

- Because popular brands result in more automatic choices, **branding ultimately makes selling easier**. Strong brands also lead to strong profits because they sell more, command a bigger market share, are less affected by market fluctuations, command a premium price and they have longevity on their side. Professor Malcolm McDonald, author of *Creating Powerful Brands* (Butterworth-Heinemann 2003), tells of one company that suspended its brand investment for one year – then spent five years trying to restore sales to previous levels. Make sure you tell all this to the finance department when they complain about brand investment.

- Brands are about value in two ways. Customers develop comfort and attachment from the way an organisation does things. Smart organisations will seek to emphasise the appealing values that exemplify the brand's personality – **the brand values**. Organisations that get this right can achieve immense success. Building values into the business will also add value onto the business. Professor McDonald adds, Proctor and Gamble paid £31 billion for Gillette in 2005, of which only £4 billion was for tangible assets such as buildings. Such is the value of the brand. Tell the finance department that too.

Building values into the business will also add value onto the business.

- Great brands are developed over time, not overnight. They are created by consistent performance and care in communicating the right sentiments to the appropriate targets. Brand awareness and brand maintenance both precede brand success. Brilliant brands do not aim to serve everybody. Successful brands focus on a specific type of customer – one they can develop an affinity with. Rolex watches aren't made for everybody, La Senza lingerie probably isn't for everybody. Brilliant brands are happy NOT to appeal to those outside their target segment – they know the customers they want and those they don't.
- Setting out deliberately to **create a brilliant brand** requires care. Ultimately, it is about starting not with what you aim to sell but with those you would want to buy it. Serious brand development should begin with, and forever after be checked by, serious understanding of the customers the brand intends to serve. Brilliant brands find out exactly what their customers want, *really want*, then provide it.
- **Brilliant brands set out to be unique**. Most have a flavour or a style or even a set of principles that helps set them apart. If you've got something to say with your brand, do it with passion. If the things that you value align with your customers' values (and they should) everything else will be easier. It can be difficult for customers to form an

It can be difficult for customers to form an opinion about a business that has none about itself.

opinion about a business that has none about itself. Being distinct also helps to avoid expensive head-on competitive clashes.

- **Consistency is key** in developing a brilliant brand. Every touch that a customer or potential customer has with your organisation is an opportunity to reinforce your brand values. Each must tell the same story and continuously nurture the same beliefs. Look at all the touch points – logo, strapline, phonecalls, letters, email, website, advertising, promotions, even invoices – and ensure that they are all in tune with your brand message. If necessary, distribute brand guidelines that set rules.
- Changing a brand (*rebranding*) or moving it away from that for which it is well known (*repositioning*) can be dangerous and should be undertaken with great care. Many brands are capable of some degree of elasticity (*brand stretch*). For example, heavy equipment giant Caterpillar also attaches its rugged, tough brand values to sturdy work and walking boots. This is successful stretch because it remains aligned with Caterpillar's brand image.
- Your brand wagon will roll easier if your employees share the journey. Ensure they are aware of and part of your brand philosophy and not merely paying lip service to it. If they don't buy into your brand, nobody else will. There are rewards here too because successful brand organisations enjoy higher than average levels of staff retention. Brilliant brands are win-win all round.

Your brand wagon will roll easier if your employees share the journey.

Summary

Be specific, appeal to the customers you want, ignore the rest. Be unique, reduce the opportunity for comparison. Be compelling, understand and meet your customers' needs so well that they don't consider going elsewhere. Be apparent, stand for something and make promises. Be trustworthy, keep your promises. Be consistent, every touch of your brand must feel the same. Be confident – and create confidence. Be above being cheap, leave penny-pinching to others. Be precious, look after your brand as your most precious asset. Be distinctive, know what you are and never compromise. Be careful – don't be shallow or fake with your brand sentiments – customers are not stupid.

Also read sections: 7; 20; 21; 31; 36

12 Measuring performance

Conscientious assessment of day-to-day activity or of marketing effort will help you identify what works, what doesn't and what next.

Intuition is a wonderful thing, but when business necks are on the line it is accountability – sure knowledge rather than woolly guesswork – that wins every time. Marketing has had a tough time of late as it strives to prove its ability to deliver quantifiable returns on investment, not to mention long-range boardroom forecasts. Modern organisations, heavily influenced by the merciless logic of digital systems, including the internet, have become focused on 'metrics' and 'return on investment'. In management generally this is not problematic, but in marketing, where the discipline is arguably half as much about creative art as it is about systematic science, matters are sometimes less cut and dried. But, just because it's tough it doesn't mean it can't be done. Measurement is wisdom.

- **Why measure?** Assessing the value gained from effort or expenditure is fundamental management practice for any organisation regardless of size or longevity. Measurement provides known factors, which translate into the ability to adjust and ultimately to control events. For example, procurement departments have long been accustomed to conducting and submitting to audit processes while marketing departments sometimes find themselves less able to do so on account of their often intangible contributions.

- **Measure what?** The assessment of organisational progress and even of non-financial goals such as consumer awareness, opinions, satisfaction and response rates are all feasible providing pre- and post-activity markers are taken for comparison, or alternatively that realistic targets are nominated at the outset. The key is to quantify the known starting position so that changes can be tracked.

The key is to quantify the known starting position so that changes can be tracked.

- **Where it gets tricky?** Assessing the value of a sales campaign is easy if the measurement criteria is simply the cost of the campaign divided by the increased revenue from the sales generated. However, there are often other, more subtle considerations that are less easily measured such as brand loyalty and customer engagement. These soft or emotional metrics are hard to directly translate into quantitative cash returns, which is why there are less marketing directors than financial directors at board level.

- **Any organisation** that hastily searches its metaphorical wallet as and when there is a marketing requirement has got it wrong – there should be a fixed-period marketing budget in place, in exactly the same way as provision is made for other running costs. Similarly, any organisation that blindly launches marketing activity without first setting some realistic expectation as to the outcome – then comparing the actual result – with the expected result, will not know whether it succeeded (so do it again) or failed (so change it).

- **Accurate measurement** – including the installation of tracking tools or predictive analytic packages – takes time and costs money. But commonsense still has a place, especially in smaller organisations where big, expensive solutions may not be appropriate. The point is this: you will manage better if you know what's going on. You will find out what's going on if you measure and evaluate.

The point is this: you will manage better if you know what's going on.

- **The hotelier's tale.** Keen to boost stagnating sales an hotelier sought marketing advice. Two important questions were raised – when are your busy or quiet periods and what is the average age of your regular customers? Neither question had ever been considered before. With no evidential foreknowledge of peaks and troughs it would be difficult to develop well-timed promotional activity. Also, many regular guests had been attending the hotel for years. It transpired that their average age had reached between 65 and 70 years. The hotel's long-established clientele were quite literally dying off. Simple, routine management assessments could have spotted both these issues before they became problems.

The hotel's long-established clientele were quite literally dying off.

- **The college tale.** The management team at one regional college were concerned over the apparent lack of public awareness relative to their newly relocated facility. Simple market research (Q. Good morning, do you know what this building is?) confirmed poor recognition of the brand and limited understanding of the facility. The marketing team stepped-up organised open events and increased press release activity. Particular efforts were made to emphasise the college's most recognisable assets (building, graphic style, slogan, student achievements) at every opportunity. Follow-up research repeating the same questions, established that public awareness had increased by 63 per cent. Result – successful campaign, accurate measurement.

- **The manufacturer's tale.** Caught in an expensive cycle of ineffective blanket promotions this company ceased its wasteful activities and spent time identifying high potential targets. Management improved the calibre of promotional methods and resolved to expend more resource per contact. They also reduced the volume of contacts to include only prime prospects. Prior to the step change, the only known measurement metric had been the annual cost of promotion. However, following the switch to tighter targeting, promotional costs fell, response rates increased, customer retention improved and, as a bonus, the new achievements will form the baseline measures for future marketing effort.

- **The simpleton's tale.** Though by no means exceptionally bright, a freelance worker possessed three useful attributes. Importantly, she was good at her job; she wasn't scared of work and could put in the hours; and, lastly, she was obsessive about counting out her day. Every chargeable hour was logged, the total hours worked each day were logged – and compared to the ones before and after. Every week's billings were logged and the end of month profit summary was compared with the equivalent position from the previous year. All this was done in a pocket notebook. Her approach might have been simple but it was far from stupid.

Her approach might have been simple but it was far from stupid.

Summary

Measuring progress and assessing effectiveness are fundamental. The keys are to: be clear about the objective; understand and record the starting point; track progress and compare the outcome against the starting point. All marketing activity should be assessed for performance. Hard metrics – return on investment – are easier to evaluate. Soft metrics – emotional gains – are more difficult to quantify and may have no visible cash payback. Where practical, look at bespoke tracking systems but don't overlook commonsense. Management data is the spinal fluid of the organisation. It can reveal what's going on and where the value is. Intuition has a place but is simply not as accountable as precise, recordable data.

Also read sections: 5; 6; 13

13 Think strategically

'There's an advantage to be had in knowing exactly why you're doing what – preferably before you do it.'

Readers blessed with onboard business Sat-nav may find it odd that this book includes a section encouraging strategic thinking, especially as most modern and progressive organisations are built around its principles. Alas, not all practitioners are equally endowed. Fifty per cent of new enterprises fail to become old enterprises; in fact, they melt away within three years of inception. The cause is invariably poor cash-flow but that is usually a symptom of a more fundamental malaise – lack of solid, practical long-term planning, an inability to join up the dots and think beyond the moment. In short, organisations go bust due to the absence of an overarching strategy that sets out where the business is heading and how it intends to get there.

- **What is strategy?** Small or new business organisations are sometimes hesitant in embracing the 'S' word. Some just don't understand it, others see it as a jargon word for plan (hey – I'm with you). Here's what the Oxford Dictionary says: *Strategy n. (1) the planning and directing of the whole operation of a campaign or war; (2) a plan or policy of this kind or to achieve something.*

- Rather like seriously large ships, serious organisations cannot be allowed to drift. Full account must be taken of what lies ahead and of the requirements for reaching the destination. Two elements are essential. Firstly, the desired goal must be clearly identified. Secondly, the means or method of achieving it must be pre-planned. Any long-term intention or defined outcome that will be met by premeditated short-term steps can be described as having a strategy.

Rather like seriously large ships, serious organisations cannot be allowed to drift.

- **What is strategic thinking?** In strategically oriented teams the long-term destination is known to all. Sudden day-to-day problems or setbacks are seen in context of the bigger picture and dealt with constructively and positively. Strategic thinkers react calmly and methodically, inspiring confidence in those around by diffusing difficulties and rejecting knee-jerk responses. Organisations that encourage a strategic approach from top to bottom are invariably impressive performers.

- **Why can't I just wing it?** The key difference between successful growth organisations and those who stand still (or worse) is the ability (or otherwise) to identify long-term ambitions that represent important stages of progress. Non-strategic organisations typically have no deep understanding of their circumstances, no plan and no systematic means of managing and overcoming problems. Consequently, they limit their own potential and increase the likelihood for failure.

> **Non-strategic organisations have no means of managing and overcoming problems.**

- **How does having a strategy help?** Hoping to succeed is not the same as planning to succeed. With no overarching structure or control process, decisions tend to become disjointed and random. There will be little or no concerted effort and no common 'glue' to keep the organisation on course. However, having a strategy in place will help ensure that routine, short-term actions fit with and contribute to the long-term intentions of the organisation, thereby reducing the potential for wasted effort and drift.

- **What does a marketing strategy do?** Ultimately, the job of marketing is to support and help deliver the ambitions contained in the business plan – i.e. to create sales, generate profit and fuel organisational growth. The marketing plan is simply an acknowledgement of specific goals and a route map that will assist their delivery. Having a marketing plan in place will co-ordinate marketing effort and help maintain a purposeful focus. Headless chickens seldom spend wisely or work productively.

> **Headless chickens seldom spend wisely or work productively.**

- **The strategic framework: Stage 1 – Analysis**. Before you can plan to move you must first analyse your position. Where are you now? What and where do you want to be in future? What are your strong or weak points? What ambitions are possible? What choices do you have? What changes might be necessary? What distractions should you ignore? What is your most valuable advantage? I realise that these points have been made elsewhere in this book – pardon the repetition – but it is a fact that the gathering and analysis of accurate information is vital to the formulation of a strategic process.

- **The strategic framework: Stage 2 – Planning.** Having assembled and considered the pertinent factors, having confirmed your intended destination, the planning stage enables the setting out of the short steps that will secure the final result. What options do you have? Are some more reliable than others? How much time is there? What resources do you have? Where can you realistically expect to reach? Which, of the products or services you offer will give you most advantages? Are any aspects of your offering likely to hold you back? How will you incorporate change? How are future markets looking? What forward steps will reduce threat and avoid risk?

- **The strategic framework: Stage 3 – Implementation.** You will now know what has to be done and how to go about it. You will have prepared to communicate your aims to all those within your organisation, especially those involved with implementing the plan, which will of course be owned by the team, not an individual – and it will have built-in assessment points to ensure that it remains on track. Final evaluation should conclude the process.

- In any business situation, in organisations large and small, a strategic approach helps control renegade or random behaviour and keeps the focus fixed firmly on the collective goal. It gives directions and provides a structure against which effective decisions can be made. The principal case for strategic thinking is this: if you first know why you are doing something – anything – you will do it better.

If first you know why you are doing something you will do it better.

Summary

Strategic thinking is a management approach that seeks to take account of any organisational situation and define the desired outcome against known facts. In so doing it helps reduce the potential for random behaviour or actions. The strategic process can be used as a pervading philosophy to crystallise the day-to-day style of individuals within the organisation or, more formally, to provide a framework for planning and attaining goals. The three stages of the strategic framework are analysis, planning and implementation. Evaluation should follow, or else be included as part of the implementation stage. Organisations that think strategically tend to progress more positively and objectively than those who do not.

Also read sections: 2; 3; 8

14 Sales and selling

The cold facts about selling fridges to Eskimos, new cars to old fools and the motives behind buying.

Canadian businessman Mel Lastman secured his place in marketing's hall of fame by selling fridges to Eskimos. In true professional style, Mel managed to successfully pedal Indesits to Inuits by first listening to their problems and understanding their needs. Though the ambient temperature in northern Canada is cold enough to preserve food, that doesn't stop animals from stealing it. Mel's fridges solved the problem and also helpfully kept the stored food from freezing rock-solid. Mel must have a relative in the UK. How else could I have gone into a car showroom, cheque book in hand, steadfastly determined to buy a low-spec used vehicle, only to emerge with a two-year finance package on a brand new, high-spec model?

- If marketing is ultimately about making a sale then the more that marketers know about how the buying or selling process works the better. The circumstances will always vary but the underlying mechanics remain consistent.

- **How do people buy?** An understanding of how people buy will help you plan how you should sell. The buying process can be broken down into five stages. (1) **The need** – recognition of a necessity, opportunity or desire. (2) **Vision** – acknowledgement of options that could satisfy the need. (3) **Acceptance** – recognition that action is required. (4) **Selection** – of the best option, person, organisation or solution. (5) **Action** – making the purchase.

An understanding of how people buy will help you plan how you should sell.

- **Why do people buy?** Most purchases are made because of: **Necessity** – my roof has collapsed and I need a new one; **Opportunity** – I can get a grant to pay for a new energy-efficient roof; **Desire** – I really fancy a 1930s style green-tiled roof. A purchase decision will also be influenced by how personal it is – a corporate purchaser will be focused on price, performance, delivery and quality (logical), whereas an individual could be driven by style, envy or imagination (emotional).

- **Why will people buy from you?** There are 12 reasons why customers might prefer to buy from you: they like what you sell; they see that it's different; they like the quality; they like the price; you are convenient; they like your store; you make it easy; you are persuasive; they like you personally; they dislike your competitor; you meet all their needs or because yours is the only store in town.

- **What will prevent people buying from you?** A sale can fail for any one of three reasons. (1) There's a difference between what you want to sell and what customers want to buy. (2) There is something wrong with your offering. (3) There is something wrong with you or your sales pitch.

A sale can fail for any one of three reasons.

- **The seven steps of a sale:** This is a typical classification – there are variations. **Planning and preparation** – knowing your offering, the competition and the prospect. **Introduction and opening** – who you are, where you're from, permission to make notes and ask questions. **Needs analysis** – empathic, open questions. Use 'what?' and 'how?' to establish the prospect's needs. **Presentation** – matching the benefits of your offering to the prospect's needs. **Overcoming objections** – flushing out, isolating and resolving sticking points. **Closing** – 'Are you happy with what we've covered? Would you like to go ahead?' **Follow-up** – conscientious after-sales contact and satisfaction check (and perfect opportunity to ask for referrals).

- **The AIDA process** is a simple but useful tool that matches sales steps according to buying motivation. It is by no means new but can still apply to personal selling and sales communication material. AIDA is an acronym that describes: **Attention** – saying, doing or showing something that captures the prospect's focus, the first impression; **Interest** – creating a link between the prospect and the offering, relevance and pertinence to their situation; **Desire** – using the benefits of the offering to demonstrate its potential to the prospect, matching the possibilities to their needs. Moving the conversation from 'maybe' to 'when'; **Action** – turning desire into reality, completing the sale.

- **Selling tips.** These steps provide a convenient reminder for successful selling. **Specialise** – don't just turn up, mean it! Treat the prospect to special attention. **Personalise** – treat each prospect as an individual. **Harmonise** – people like people like them. **Analyse** – establish the prospect's needs. **Emotionalise** – paint a picture of the possibilities. **Rationalise** – support the vision with factual benefits. **Empathise** – never lie, tell the

Never lie, tell the 'available' truth but tailor it to the prospect's needs.

'available' truth but tailor it to the prospect's needs. **Mobilise** – don't just discuss it, conclude with a sale.

- **Important points.** Sales performance consultant Paul Narraway highlights two fundamental issues. *'Needs analysis is absolutely vital. You shouldn't do ANYTHING until you have fully identified the prospect's real needs. The second point is that people buy from people. In any interpersonal situation the single most important feature is the relationship – no chemistry, no sale.'*

No chemistry, no sale.

- **Some dos and don'ts.** Do focus the prospect on potential gains by asking what the effects of your offering could be worth to them. Do minimise any negative response to your price by keeping the prospect focused on the value of its benefits. Do treat objections as possible deal-makers by saying 'If I can resolve this point for you will you place an order?' Don't use the words 'why' or 'but' during the needs analysis stage – they imply challenge. Don't openly knock the competition – give the prospect the ammunition to do it for you.

Summary

Look at the pattern of how people buy – it will help you plan how you should sell. The reasons why people buy are necessity, opportunity or desire. Look again at the 12 reasons why a buyer will choose to buy from you. Three reasons for a failed sale are: your offering is not matched to customer needs; there is a problem with the offering; or there is a problem with you. The classic seven steps to a sale are: planning and preparation; introduction and opening; questioning; presentation; overcoming objections; closing; and follow-up. Accurate needs analysis is vital. AIDA – attention, interest, desire and action – is old, but still effective.

Also read sections: 6; 19; 24; 49

CHAPTER THREE

Setting your house in order

In this chapter:

15. **Winning the name game** – is yours a great name or a great shame?
16. **Logo, badge and icon** – the rules that will help you form a winning symbol
17. **Strapping straplines** – the importance of having a mouse that roars
18. **Stretching your marketing budget** – making every penny count
19. **Queue alone** – improve your chances by being the only contender

15 Winning the name game

'The name of your organisation or products can be the first touch point for buyers – best ensure it's a winner not a sinner.'

Abstract names such as Google may not mean much but they are memorable. Obvious puns such as The Perfect Plaice or Cutting Crew suggest businesses of a certain type and size. Giant corporates with momentum can cope with BAT or GEC, while family or personal pride is an issue for the likes of Mars, and Bob's Motors. Partnerships like Fortnum & Mason play it straight, though descriptive monikers like The Hire Shop play it straighter still. There are those rooted to their birthplace like North Eastern Trailers and those who are made for the internet, such as Screedpumps.co.uk. Finally, consider those who like to link what they do with how they do it – AbleGlaze and Budget Rent-a-Car as examples. The possibilities are truly endless.

- According to a survey carried out by Yell, 82 per cent of us agree that **businesses need a noticeable name**. That said, 26 per cent said they went for the first name that popped into their heads and 43 per cent chose to follow their own judgement rather than take advice. This might explain the 37 per cent who would now like to change their name. Your business name can often be the gateway towards that vital first impression – so it is important. Unsurprisingly, the soft drink named 'Yum Yum' failed to catch on but positively fizzed when renamed Coca-Cola. A similar change of destiny affected the young Mortimer Mouse when his creator decided that Mickey Mouse sounded friendlier.

- If you are naming a new venture **think ahead** to avoid future problems. Do you want to appear innovative or traditional? Do you want your name to incorporate and advertise what you do? Is it wise to name the business or its products after yourself or your family or even your geographic location, any of which could prove to be an unhelpful anchor in the future? Consider what happened to all those millennium organisations called 'something 2000'. Do you want memorable, distinctive, weird, or just easy to say and spell?

If you are naming a new venture think ahead.

- Your corporate name need not be the same as your trading name or individual product names. For example, Mars Incorporated controls

Pedigree Petfoods, Uncle Ben's Rice and a host of successful products including M&M's, Snickers and Mars Bars – but is mentioned by name on just one. Using a non-specific corporate name can be helpful in supporting future brand diversification, as in the case of Virgin: Atlantic; Media; Money; Trains; Radio; and so on.

> **You are unlikely ever to drive an Audi Pardner!**

- The British do seem to love a **commercial pun** – Tan-fastic and the Cod Father are nice examples. Our American cousins are hot on the case too with offerings such as Al Bums, Ewe 'n' Me and Hair Force One. Big organisations tend to avoid pun names – so you are unlikely to ever drive an Audi Pardner!

> **Eastern Airlines went bust because nobody realised they also flew north, south and west.**

- **Common oversights** can limit the appeal of a commercial name. These include: confusion with another entity (Continental Airlines and Continental Tyres); being too specific (Eastern Airlines went bust because nobody realised they also flew north, south and west); not being specific enough (Road Reviver – a non-spill pet water bowl); meaningless initials (BMX, GBH, APH); and anything that invokes recollections or something unpopular (D'eath or Cyclone Holidays).
- Once an organisation gains mass it automatically gains credibility and becomes an unquestioned part of the commercial landscape. Here the name itself is less important because the brand has become familiar. **For newer arrivals**, however, the journey is just beginning. Long names, geographic names, odd names, quirky spelling and the implications of alphabetical directories suddenly need to be thought through more carefully.
- **Addresses** are less important for big batters but can be an issue for smaller organisations. For example, Magnificent Machinery would carry less clout if the first line of their address was 'Barely Works'. Similarly, any one-man band trying to appear much larger would fail to impress with an address such as 'The Smith Corporation, No 42A Chrysanthemum Drive . . .'.
- You can enhance adoption of your name by making it friendly. For example, Indian Food entrepreneur Tiny Deol launched her weight-conscious label under the instantly friendly name 'CurrySlim'. It states exactly what benefit it will deliver and does so quickly and without a hint of negativity. Still on the same theme, diet maestros Obesity

Lifeline found instant success when they changed their product name to 'LighterLife', which is both more promising and more welcoming than their former brand handle.

> **One organisation adopted the name of a murderer.**

- Faux Latin and names borrowed from mythology (Aventis, Veriton, Telegent) provide gravitas and implied longevity. They also helpfully suggest respectable size. But there are two cautions. Firstly, if you intend to trade abroad do check that your name is not somehow inappropriate. Secondly, if you borrow from mythology do check the pedigree behind the name you select. One organisation adopted the name of a minor Greek deity only to later discover that their hero had been a murderer.
- Consider the internet before settling on a final choice for a corporate name. Check that your selection is foolproof and uses standard spelling. Key it into an online search to check for unexpected meanings. Ask others to write it and see if common errors emerge. Check that you can secure an appropriate domain – remember you don't have to use your full organisational name as your domain. Remember too that separated words can develop an entirely different meaning when joined up – witness www.expertsexchange.com (Experts Exchange) and www.speedofart.com (Speed of Art). Ooops indeed!

Summary

Commercial names are important. They can help you stand out and be remembered. They can begin shaping customer expectations too. Don't rush in – look at options and involve those you expect to reach in the selection process. Above all, think ahead – how might the organisation or the name seem in five years? Remember that your corporate name need not be the same as your product or trading name. Avoid puns that might wear thin in time, avoid being either over- or under-specific and avoid names that might have a different meaning for others. There are rules that apply to UK Business Names – check with Companies House *www.companieshouse.gov.uk*.

Also read sections: 13; 17; 21

16 Logo, badge and icon

'There are a variety of ways of describing the brand icon and a variety of gains from having a winning design.'

The job of your logo is to get you recognised quickly amongst the visual avalanche of similar organisations, products and causes. A simple logo can proclaim the coolest casino in Las Vegas, highlight the hottest hamburgers in Hamburg, separate the men from the boys in the pub and signpost which loo is your loo anywhere on earth. Dare to whip off your kit in a phone box without revealing the super 'S' logo and you'll probably be arrested. Logos do it all and a good one is often defined not by what it contains but what it leaves out. For example, the McDonald's logo makes its case without showing any hint of a burger. Logos can sometimes pass unnoticed, but look closely and you'll find there's a lot to consider.

> **The logo acts as the cornerstone of a brand's visual identity.**

- **The word logo** comes from the Greek word *logotypos*. In current usage it refers to the symbol, marque, icon, trademark, emblem, sign or badge that visually represents or identifies an organisation or its products. Its job is to act as graphic shorthand or as a signature that both defines and acts as the cornerstone of a brand's visual identity. In the same way that road traffic signs encapsulate a meaning without the need for a written explanation, a logo helps us to quickly identify one entity from another.
- **Who or what needs a logo?** Everyone apparently – organisations, super heroes, products, campaigns, bands, films, the military, food, TV shows, newspapers – logos are everywhere, even in the middle of nowhere footpaths are denoted by . . . a logo. There are even countries that have their own logo.
- Although it is often the familiar feature of a brand, the logo is not the brand itself. Logo designs can be broadly categorised into three types: symbolic – a shape or abstract icon such as the Nike swoosh; metaphoric – an illustrative depiction, for example, the Michelin tyre man; typographic – either spelling out a word or using abbreviated letter forms as in Sainsbury's or VW. Whatever form it takes, the golden rule is that **a logo should be unique**.
- Thanks to its iconic logo Coca-Cola can be identified almost anywhere on earth, even where the words themselves are changed to suit

different alphabets or languages. The Red Cross and the Red Crescent are also recognised globally and require no descriptors. Christians have used the simple fish motif (Ichthys) since the first century AD. Another ancient symbol that has seen interesting times is the Swastika, which, despite its recent history, began as an Indian icon of good luck.

The Swastika began as an Indian icon of good luck.

- The current top ten **most admired logos** according to *www.good-logo.com* are: Stüssy, Apple, WorldWildlife Fund, BMW, Coca-Cola, Batman, Volkswagen, Disney Entertainment, Nike and Adidas. Interestingly, the Nike swoosh logo earned its designer, Carolyn Davidson, $35 – not a lot for what later became one of the world's most successful designs. Nike thought so too and later returned to Carolyn with a more appropriate expression of their thanks.
- In recent years there has been a shift away from the flat or 'spot' colour approach to logo design that has been anchored by the limitations of print-based reproduction. The growing influence of the internet has opened new possibilities. More intricate, multi-coloured 3D designs complete with transparent or half-tone touches are now the order of the day. Swooshes too are now becoming less popular, having given way to waves and flowing shapes. These trends also reveal the growing impact of digital printing, in which the use of multiple colours is unrestricted.
- **A logo should be representative** of the values of the product or organisation it represents and relevant to those who will view it. It should be clear and retain its clarity regardless of size or medium. It should work in colours and in black only – and not turn into a blob if photocopied. It should reproduce reliably and without problems, regardless of media choice. It should above all be unique, not a pastiche of something else. If you use clip-art you will not be unique or be investing in your brand assets, nor will you be able to secure trademark protection.
- There is no need for a logo design to explain or depict too literally what the organisation does. If a firm produces dentures, for example, it does not follow that its logo should include teeth – no more than the Ford logo should have wheels. Colour can sometimes become a technical issue because print colours are not the same as screen colours. The final outcome

If a firm produces dentures it does not follow that its logo should include teeth.

should include a suite of logos in different file formats for varied needs.

- The logo is often the endorsement of the brand and it should be **treated with respect**. Look at the way enlightened organisations treat their symbol. You might notice an exclusion zone of clear space around the logo that enables it to work well – the dignity and confidence of a logo will diminish if it becomes crowded by other matter. Wise designers provide a set of usage guidelines that stipulate simple rules for how the symbol should be positioned and deployed.
- You are not legally obliged to register or 'patent' your logo but it can be wise to do so. The protection thus afforded will prevent others from imitating your organisation or product. For details see the Intellectual Property Office *www.ipo.gov.uk* or the Institute of Trade Mark Attorneys *www.itma.org.uk*. Before you appoint a designer to produce a logo, clarify who will own the intellectual property rights to the design.

> **If you plan to one day sell your business you should consider trademark protection.**

Summary

The logo is the hallmark that endorses all that an organisation or movement represents. It should be clear, consistent, legible and unique. It should also work in varied media at varied sizes. It does not need to provide an all inclusive visual metaphor for what an organisation or product is or does. A logo can, as part of the brand, acquire a capital value of its own – consider this carefully if you plan to one day sell your business. Consider trademark protection too. Incidentally, colours, jingles, smells, gestures and distinctive sounds that provide corporate identification in the same way as a logo can also be protected as trademarks.

Also read sections: 9; 11; 17; 21; 22; 45

17 Strapping straplines

'Those often delightful yet frequently under-exploited miniature adverts that can achieve so much without breaking the bank – truly the mouse that roars!'

Not to be confused with an organisation's mission statement, the strapline is often seen alongside the brand icon, expressing some aspect of the brand promise. Consumer trust in a brand can be more rapidly established when viewers are able to identify and evaluate what the organisation can do for them. The strapline invariably provides a better opportunity to explain or promote the brand offering than the logo itself. Therefore it performs a vital role in explaining the offer and winning friends. Usually straplines are strategically focused and summarise the organisation's long-term positioning. However, there is no rule that says they can't also be used tactically and even changed periodically providing it is relevant to do so and in a way that is succinct – not an essay.

- **The strapline is** the short statement that often follows a brand name or logo. It can also be described as tag-line, sig-line, slogan or end-line. Its job can be to create interest, to explain or simply to win friends. Many successful straplines began as part of an ad campaign and were adopted as permanent assets. Others were never intended to be anything more than slogans.

- The rationale for the strapline is to influence – to fix the essence of the brand or its services in the mind of the viewer. Because of their brevity, straplines can present a belief or a sales principle in a way that is easy to digest and remember. The strapline is, in effect, **a mini headline** that says 'if you don't remember anything else, remember this because it sums up what we can do for you'.

> **The strapline is a mini headline that sums up what you can do.**

- You don't need to be a major brand name to use a strapline. They work for any organisation, any business or any product. For example, 'Newcastle – passionate about regeneration' or 'Barry's Burgers – every bite delights'. The most important features of a successful strapline are that it should be both **simple and memorable**. Make it short, make it sweet.

- Straplines can **work in various ways**. They might simply describe the offering, for example, Polo – 'the mint with the hole', or they can include a benefit, as with 'No one's quicker than a Quick-Fit Fitter'. They can promote the quality of a product or service, for example, the University of Essex – 'Educational excellence on your doorstep'. You might even use a strapline to create intrigue when most readers don't have a clue what you are saying – 'Vorsprung durch technik'. Or you can add a touch of humour – 'Hexham Jail – welcoming guests for over 600 years'. You can inspire, as did Nancy Reagan's 'Just say No'. You might even influence common culture as Ronseal did with 'Does exactly what it says on the tin'.

'Does exactly what it says on the tin'.

- You can use a strapline to differentiate your offering from its competitors and to support your marketing strategy; for example, Coca-Cola – 'it's the real thing' suggests the Coke drinkers don't accept substitutes and thereby that Coke is the number one brand in its sector. Similarly, Heinz's 'Beanz Meanz Heinz' states a strong claim that's hard to follow.
- Sometimes straplines can become so recognisable that they can be used as a stand-alone statement or headline; for example, Nike's 'Just do it' needs no accompanying corporate blurb. Other extensions could include using the strapline to endorse an advert or a news release.
- **To create a strapline**, start by writing the words or phrases that define and surround your offering. Avoid technical descriptions and focus only on the kind of words your customers will understand. For example, Smiths Dentists might write: dentist; painless; excellence; mouth; gums; attractive; easy; friendly; extracting; filling; smile; cosmetic; decay; treatment; cost; oral; helpful; breath; health; age; cleaning; check-up; crown; halitosis and so on. There's no pattern, this is just a brain dump. It often pays to come back to this process several times over a few days.

Start by writing the words or phrases that define your offering.

- Discounting the negative words such as pain or halitosis and operational words such as treatment or filling, begin to assemble short sentences that incorporate the words that will interest your customers – attractive, easy, friendly, care, best, smile, helpful, etc. Remember that the aim is not to offer a precise technical definition of the offering but to summarise the experience your customers would like. For example: Open wide for friendly service; Service with a smile: Looking after you and your teeth; Plenty to smile about; Oral care at its best; Perfect chums for teeth and gums.

- Live with your statements for a few days and concentrate on shortening those that work best. From the selection above you could end up with 'Plenty to smile about' and 'Oral care at its best'. Once you have a shortlist it's easy to ask a few trusted customers to comment. This example is a fictitious dental practice but the same process can be used to create a memorable strapline for any organisation or product.

- Providing it is done well a strapline can become **the simplest, most cost-effective advert** you will ever create. But as with all things, don't be bashful about seeking professional help if you find the DIY route a struggle. Don't feel obliged to be humorous or clever. Simple is often best. An awkward or uninteresting company name can be improved by a factual accompanying strapline. For example, the law firm Crooke, Rippov & Blagger could be usefully softened by the addition of – 'Family Solicitors since 1932'.

The simplest, most cost-effective advert you will ever create.

Summary

Word for word a good strapline could easily become the most memorable – and therefore most valuable – advert you have. Your strapline can be used to say something about a specific aspect of your product or services, or alternatively to make a general statement about the way you do business. Your strapline should be a summary not a story. The process for developing a strapline has two stages: first you have to decide what to say – what single, important point do you want to convey about your organisation? Stage two is all about boiling it down, removing any impurities until you are left with a succinct one-liner that should sit near your name or logo.

Also read sections: 9; 11; 16; 18

18 Stretching your marketing budget

A tight marketing budget might present a challenge but it shouldn't render you powerless.

If it is to be done properly, marketing, like any other management discipline, requires time, effort and inevitably some degree of financial commitment. But the fact is that many organisations simply cannot afford the things they would most like to have. Typically those that see marketing as an occasional emergency event (rather than an ongoing process) are usually the ones who feel discomfort at the sudden need to find and spend money. The simple solution is to treat marketing the same way as the rent or the electricity – as part of the running costs. But we digress. The need for marketing without the benefit of deep pockets may not be a perfect ideal but it is achievable.

- **Reduce wasted opportunities**. Business cards, email footers, phone answer-messages, compliment slips, address labels, envelopes, invoices and packaging all provide promotional opportunities. Most business cards are printed in two colours, one side only – why not put a mini-advert or sales message on the back too? Vehicles also present a fantastic opportunity to get your message across – and there's no need to limit your message to a name and a strapline.
- **Target accurately.** Expert Andrew Chalk recommends keeping your marketing focused on the best customer opportunities. This will help you achieve optimum results with minimum wasted effort. Target only the customers you want, promote only via the media that reaches them. Set goals and measure your success.

Target only the customers you want.

- **Nurture a good reputation**. Cultivate a natural reason for customers to select you – something that distinguishes your organisation from others. Seize this point of difference and emphasise it. Proclaim it, remind people about it, bring it to life and turn it into a brand belief. Transform it into a slogan and display it alongside your logo. British Airways is still known as 'the world's favourite airline' even though the slogan was dropped in 2001. Reputations can be powerful, long-lasting and free.

- **Look after good customers**. Every sale that you don't have to go out and win saves you time, effort and money. Identify your best customers – those who are the least problematic, the most profitable, or even the most pleasant if that's what matters to you personally – and look after them. Make sure you stay in touch and give their needs your fullest personal priority. The lifetime value of a star customer can be phenomenal. It's a fact that loyal customers rarely leave a business relationship because of price but because they feel ignored or taken for granted.

> Every sale that you don't have to win saves time, effort and money.

- **Promote with care.** The quickest way to blow a hole in your marketing budget is to use mainstream media that forces you to shout louder (and spend more) to compete. Use simpler ideas and communicate directly where possible. Hire a marketing 'creative' for an hour and brainstorm low-cost ideas. For example, a foldable, branded paper plane template could keep contacts amused for hours. Or, use classified ad space (cheap) rather than display ad space (costly).

- **Seek referrals**. Word of mouth (WOM) is actually a more potent means of promotion than advertising, and it's free! WOM is easy to instigate – providing you get into the habit of asking. Approach customers or suppliers and make the most of networking. Naturally you must be willing to take the time and trouble to return the compliment occasionally. A good customer or supplier will genuinely be pleased to see you benefit from a recommendation.

> Word of mouth is more potent than advertising and it's free!

- **Be more creative.** If your organisation is to be noticed it must first attract attention. For example, press or media relations can often be managed internally – perhaps with the help of a 'how to' course. Develop a creative angle that will interest the press or radio. Alternatively, send prospecting letters out with a sweet treat attached – this will get you noticed. One IT provider sends his clients a fortnightly collection of humorous or thought-provoking photographs by email. This is not 'hard sell' – which is probably why it works.

- **Turn your workforce into a salesforce.** Turn your staff into a marketing department for an hour or two each week. They can research, send prospecting letters, make customer phone calls and attend networking events. They will value the opportunity to represent the business and the net result for you will be more contacts – five people each sending five prospecting letters per week adds up to 100 contacts each month! Make sure you energise the process with incentives.

> **Five people sending five prospecting letters per week adds up to 100 contacts.**

- **Leverage supplier support.** Website builders often include their company name or a link on sites they have built. Similarly, it is not uncommon to see a brochure or catalogue that identifies those who designed it or printed it. Whilst it is reassuring that these suppliers are keen to publicly endorse their work, the fact remains that you might be providing them with free advertising. What can they do for you in return?

- **Become a recognised expert.** Providing of course you know your business and are happy to strut your stuff in public, there's no reason why you can't become a luminary for your industry. Time spent creating an interesting presentation will often win you an audience eager to learn from your experience – and keen to discuss a project afterwards perhaps?

- **Make use of the web**. The internet offers great opportunities to reach wide audiences for comparatively little outlay. You can attract interest by offering tips, you can open a blog, register with online directories and with the main search engines. Find a web-marketing expert and pay for one hour's worth of advice and suggested options before you decide which methods suit you.

Summary

Look after the housekeeping first. Make sure you gain as much exposure as possible using the tools and people you already work with. Avoid looking cheap, unconfident or homemade – all of which can send negative signals. Stylish and creative use of one colour can often be more effective than poorly focused use of four colours, saving the cost of three. Reputation and customer care cost nothing yet the results they can achieve could be priceless. Every existing customer that remains loyal is one less that you will have to find by your marketing efforts.

Also read sections: 6; 10; 19; 38; 47

19 Queue alone

> *The shape, size, quality and price of your widgets will matter less if they are the only widgets in the room.*

Consistent marketing success is inextricably linked to the calibre of its planning and on the way an organisation differentiates itself from its rivals in order to win greater sales. Usually this means carefully balancing the 4Ps – product, price, promotion, place – to make the offering attractive, available and profitable. But these are strategic measures that, whilst they are valid, can sometimes blind us to simpler, more streetwise solutions. The aim of this section is to remind us to look simply at the potential of gaining a position that helps us to avoid the competitive crowd and become the obvious customer choice – preferably by being the sole choice. This is not complex marketing strategy but simple commonsense. Success is often about being different enough, and bold enough, to walk away from the herd.

- On my wife's birthday a handwritten, coloured envelope arrived by mail. In fact there were quite a few but this one turned out to be special. The envelope contained a high quality birthday card which was personalised with my wife's name. Inside it was a £5.00 gift voucher and personal best wishes from a shop where she has an account. This was unexpected and very well done – it had great impact.
- Rather than spend fortunes promoting themselves alongside their competitors one firm of London solicitors organised a high quality art exhibition. There were no sales pitches just rapport building. Though the 'sell' was soft it was convivial and highly effective. Best of all, there were no competitors there to spoil things.
- Before you send another prospecting letter consider the likelihood of your envelope looking exactly the same as other hopefuls. Think of ways to deliver or present it in a way that sets you apart. For example, you could use a brightly coloured postal tube, or a huge yellow envelope; use courier delivery. Or you could deliver on the weekend or attach it to a gift. Whatever else you do, do your utmost to be different.

Whatever else you do, do your utmost to be different.

- Before you pay to advertise in a trade journal consider writing for it instead. This will bring you credibility and recognition as an expert.

Similarly, you could offer to give a presentation at a business event. You might not be the sole widget maker in the room but you will be the only one with the microphone.

- As an alternative from trying to schmooze their prospects during office hours (when they are either busy or distracted) one wise insurance agency makes use of a private box at the local soccer stadium. This works particularly well given that most of their prospects are male and available on Saturdays.
- Of the four hire car desks at Newcastle Airport only one was consistently busy. Why? Because they had done a deal with a popular airline and promised special discounts for its inbound passengers. They were not the only car hire desk in the room but they were the only one whose commonsense kept them one step ahead of their rivals.

Of the four hire car desks at Newcastle Airport only one was consistently busy. Why?

- There must be dozens of different types of potato crisps and corn snacks. But there is only one brand that consistently flies off the shelf at weekends and party times. The reason? This star brand is the only one that features a resealable tube pack rather than a conventional bag. Being different makes you easy to choose.
- Consider the guy that volunteered to drive a potential buyer to a business event. Sure enough, when the buyer entered the room a mob of eager wannabees surrounded him with a barrage of leaflets and business cards. They were all wasting their time. The business had already been earmarked for the polite, helpful and less pushy guy that had done the driving.

When the buyer entered the room a mob of eager wannabees surrounded him. They were all wasting their time.

- If you habitually like to make a 'Thank you' gesture to your key customers at Christmas you could do worse than to observe these two suggestions. Firstly, don't do the same tired old thing as everyone else. Secondly, don't do it at the same time as everyone else – especially if your gift could disappear into an anonymous stockpile of identical offerings. The same offering presented personally and sincerely in mid-January will have much more impact.
- Customers are real people too. Take the time and the trouble to meet key contacts for lunch occasionally. Don't insult them (and yourself) by turning the event into an obvious business 'butter-up'. Aim instead

for a mutually pleasurable time and get to know the person rather than their role. Providing you can be honest and genuine there is no harm in becoming friends too.

- The internet is changing the way we shop. We are becoming less reliant on building an individual personal rapport with a helpful sales assistant and more focused on obtaining the commodity at the right price. Though human personality is all but removed from the process, those websites that focus on the principles of human trust and rapport tend to succeed more than those who do not.
- At the Glastonbury music festival Orange Mobile provided free mobile phone recharge facilities. There were no strings attached and no heavy sales pitch but the friendly gesture was perfectly pitched to the needs of the customer and made a big, long-lasting, impression. Selling isn't always about sales.

Selling isn't always about sales.

Summary

Promoting your way to a competitive advantage can be expensive and time-consuming. There are alternative ways of making an impact. In a world rammed full of commercial stratagems and the increasing priority of process over personality, taking the time to differentiate yourself on a human level can be both refreshing and rewarding. This philosophy is not about selling overtly, though sales may well result. It is about getting closer to your clients by treating them as people, not as targets. It is also about being more creative, more expert and more trustworthy than your rivals – but only if you can be sincere too.

Also read sections: 11; 14; 21; 50

CHAPTER FOUR

Sales and communication nuggets

In this chapter:

20. **Effective communication** – because if it fails to influence . . . it fails
21. **Creating impact** – stand out by being outstanding
22. **Graphic design** – don't bother looking good, look great!
23. **Website design** – just the same, but totally different
24. **Features, benefits, action** – saying what it is, what it does, how to get it

20 Effective communication

'Wise marketers steer clear of the lowerarchy of dependency by recognising, not underestimating, the value of communication.'

Consider what goes into a marketing campaign: initial research and analysis; product development and testing; strategic planning; positioning; budget calculations. It amounts to an absolute tsunami of effort. But despite all this high falutin' foreplay, ultimately the difference between success and failure can rest on the way the offering is introduced to the buyer. In other words, it all comes down to the effectiveness (or otherwise) of your communication. All organisations, regardless of their size, should recognise the importance of communication if they seek to be clearly understood and to win friends and allies, not to mention customers. And don't make the mistake of thinking you have no competitors – everything else with a message vying for your customers' attention, regardless of what it is selling, is your competition.

Everything with a message vying for your customers' attention is your competition.

- **Consider language.** Your terms and expressions may not be the same as your customers'. Do they really want training and development programmes or do they want a brighter future? Do they want ISAs, PEPs and PIPs or do they want a secure nest egg? Do they want something that boasts 'total maximised efficiency' or do they just want to know that it works? Language can camouflage your intentions and obstruct success. It can also inadvertently position your offering; for example, the word consultant sounds grand (but expensive), while alternatives like guide or mentor are friendlier.

The lowerarchy of communication dependency

- **Consider focus.** Are customers merely buying your widget or does it meet a deeper desire that you could harness in your communication. Are AA and RAC members paying for car repairs or the reassurance of having a guardian angel within reach? Do solicitors sell legal advice or confidence? Do Cartier buyers just want jewellery or is exclusivity part of their motive? Don't just sell your widget. Find out the need it really meets and target that.

- **Consider tone.** How do you like to be spoken to? Do you enjoy being shouted at? Patronised? Bamboozled? Threatened? Think carefully about the tone of voice your organisation uses to woo customers. You can 'shout at' or 'talk at' or 'talk to' but you might find it most useful to talk 'with'. A conversational writing style wins friends.

Do you enjoy being shouted at? Patronised? Bamboozled? Threatened?

- **Consider interest.** We 'feel' interest way before our conscious mind analyses the value of becoming interested. This is why pictures and the overall visual impression that a design offers can be crucial in attracting attention and unlocking emotions – often before a single word is read. Merely setting down your good intentions using beard-growingly verbose passages of text is not the best way to make your point. Make visual first impressions count.

- **Consider headlines.** Words make powerful tools. A good headline can suggest the entire story or enough of it to encourage the reader to stay with you long enough to get into the detail. Look at the difference between: poster headlines – short and sharp; direct marketing headlines – longer, more explanatory; press headlines – urgent or dramatic; promotional headlines – benefit led. Never go with the first headline you think of; write five or six then pick the best.

- **Consider type.** Consumers know the difference between skilfully and poorly used type, so they can form a view on your professional credibility. Unless you know about type and how to use it, avoid the following common pitfalls. Do not: use more than three fonts on one communication; put headlines in capitals; ram type out to the edges of the page or screen; over-do the use of initial capitals at the beginning of words; use ampersands [&] in running text. Do not use Times Bold for everything; cram the line spacing; use decorative display fonts for text. But do take notice of how professional typographers and designers use type and learn from them.

MY BUSINESS IS CRAP!

- **Consider clarity.** Be clear before being clever. One well-intended, but otherwise disastrous business letter began with the headline MY BUSINESS IS CRAP! Apparently, when (if) the reader took the trouble to wade through the heavy rhetoric to the bottom of the page CRAP was explained to mean Creative, Resourceful, Active, Professional. All very entertaining and clever, providing the reader stayed to the end. Few did.
- **Consider simplicity.** Use a single-minded 'proposition' and focus the reader on one thing at a time. Distil your arguments or emphasis points down to the shortest possible length. Don't be tempted to shoehorn too many offers or explanations at once. Less IS invariably more, especially online. Build your communication on these steps: (1) Hook – gain attention. (2) Explain – benefits and features. (3) Confirm – reiterate the benefits. (4) Nudge – lead the reader to act. (5) The Columbo – that final killer PS.
- **Consider impact.** Try the Party Bore Test. Read your marketing text and count how many references you make about yourself or your organisation. This includes every 'we', 'us', 'me', 'our' and 'my'. Now count how many references you make in favour of your reader – you, your and you're. Add up the totals. Ideally, your text should refer to your targets far more than to you.
- **Consider definition.** Always define your message carefully before you attempt to communicate it. Use these check points: Does my message make clear sense? Will it inspire interest? Does it seem like it comes from a friend? Will it be emotionally relevant to my target? Is it likely to get them to do what I want? Does it dignify and support the values of my brand? Have I tested it? Could it be better? How will it compare with the efforts of the enemy?

How will it compare with the efforts of the enemy?

Summary

In commercial and competitive situations poor communication is not an option. Ordinarily, your customers and potential customers will not go out of their routine way to find you or learn what you do. The onus is with you to break the silence, to say something that gains their attention and leads to a positive response. You need to attract your customers and tell them clearly and concisely what it is that you have and why they should get excited about it. Finally, you need to do all this at least as well as, if not better than, your competitors.

Also read sections: 10; 21; 22; 24; 26

21 Creating impact

The best way to stand out is to be outstanding – making a strong impression can put you ahead of the game.

Actor Oliver Reed was to be interviewed by Michael Parkinson. Reed arrived in the studio completely naked except for green Wellington boots! Businessman Victor Kyam could have said, 'I recommend this razor'. Instead he announced, 'I liked the product so much, I bought the company'. Concerned that a customer had a few minor niggles with service, a hotel manager took the bill for the entire week's stay and reduced it by half. One distraught husband, on learning of his wife's extra-marital affair, offered her for sale on eBay – including her photograph and a full description of her exploits. The point linking each of the above anecdotes is impact. If you want to be noticed you must dare to be different.

- **Impact in marketing** is often a case of putting aside old habits in favour of consideration. There is no excuse for (or point in) habitually churning out communication that has little effect. Impact is necessary to penetrate the curtain of competitor activity that can blind and deafen your intended customers. The good news is that impact is a commodity available to all.

The good news is that impact is a commodity available to all.

- **Stopping to think has impact.** Waiting rooms are a challenge for marketers. One example contained a riot of communication – more than 50 small posters, a similar number of leaflet dispensers and two community notice boards. The owners of all these messages had added layer upon layer of noise without stepping back to think. A ceiling mobile, a floor graphic or a digital display could each have provided greater impact.

- **Smart strategies have impact.** Intelligent thinking helped transform the humble English pilchard into a high performing gourmet commodity. Clever market positioning hauled the product upscale by playing on memories of carefree holidays and alfresco cooking. Evocative packaging helped complete the vision and elevated the merely average to become the very special. The fish remained the same but its new image changed everything.

The fish remained the same but its new image changed everything.

- **Audacity has impact.** A London Ad agency arranged a meeting with senior British Rail management. On arrival the BR team were rudely told to wait. The delay went unexplained, much to the annoyance of the busy visitors. They were eventually offered meagre refreshments – lukewarm coffee and boring, tired sandwiches. The wait continued. Finally, as tempers began to fray, the plot was revealed. The agency had deliberately staged the delay to demonstrate how British Rail customers were treated. The BR team took the hint and customer care went on to the agenda.

- **Creativity has impact.** Imagine your task is to promote Dubai as a brilliant place to work and play. Your target is London's business community. You could put ads in the commuter newspapers or financial press, but that's a bit predictable. Alternatively, you could have a BIG idea! You could develop your message – the grass is greener in Dubai – then bring it to life. You could customise a fleet of London taxicabs, covering their roofs with bright green astroturf. You could send them in convoy through the locale of your target audience. Naturally you would ensure that every influential magazine and newspaper was supplied with great pictures and the full story – and that's exactly what happened.

- **Simplicity has impact.** Adman David Ogilvy famously increased sales for Rolls Royce, not by saying these are great cars, nor by waxing technical about top speed, nor by playing the predictable prestige trump card. Ogilvy's Ad focused on a small detail that conveyed the whole message. He wrote, 'At 60mph the loudest noise in this new Rolls Royce comes from the electric clock'.

- **Colour has impact**. In a study for the US Digital Printing Council, Romano and Broudy examined direct mail responses. They found that a black-and-white mailing averaged responses of 0.46 per cent while a fully coloured mailing increased response to 46 per cent. Using full colour and the recipient's name increased responses by 135 per cent over the black-and-white test piece. Adding personalised database information about the recipient yielded response rates about 500 per cent above the test piece.

> **Using full colour and the recipient's name increased responses by 135 per cent.**

- **Being unpredictable has impact.** Corporate slide presentations can be dull. Invariably each slide looks exactly and tediously the same as the last, and the next. All that might vary is the exact number of bullet points on each. The result? Boredom, disengagement and poor retention. However, if you dispose of the homogenous corporate styling and permit individuality, if you introduce each new bullet point separately, if you stop titles revealing the full story, then your slides will become more interesting and more effective.

- **Drama has impact.** A tall office block, suddenly something hurtles downwards, exploding into fragments way below. Then another . . . it's a computer . . . there's another. At street level there's a huge skip filled with dead computers. Crash! There's another. As a viewer of this commercial you're drawn into it. You're bursting to know who is destroying these valuable computers. Then all is revealed. It's time to dump all your old stuff and make way for brilliant new technology. Simply saying as much without the compelling footage would not have worked.

At street level there's a huge skip filled with dead computers.

- **Dumping habits has impact.** Tired and predictable marketing seldom works. The most effective method may not be the most obvious. The cheapest route is not necessarily the best and a co-ordinated mix of tools usually works better than a one-off. Your logo, your face, your factory, your favourite colour, your pride and joy, your jargon, and your preferences might not be of the least interest to your target audience. ALWAYS put what interests and engages them first.

Summary

Impact gets you and your message noticed and remembered. It is available to all and does not require big budgets – just effort. Impact is not necessarily about being bigger, bolder or louder – just smarter. The key to achieving impact is first to thoroughly understand your goal and then to try and approach it in a different way. Dump old habits and open your mind to new possibilities. Make your message simple and find ways to present it that inspire interest. Learn to separate the average from the brilliant – and aim to be brilliant. Nobody ever got successful by being mediocre.

Also read sections: 13; 22; 24; 26

22 Graphic design

'The secret of persuasive visual appeal is not to settle for looking good when you have the opportunity to look great.'

Broadly speaking, design can solve practical problems, challenge emotions or simply distinguish one widget from another. Think about your clothes, your car, your furniture or even your kettle. Beyond their functional qualities each of these items attracted you and appealed enough to prompt you to buy them. More specifically, the purpose of graphic design, in the context of marketing, is to attract, define and explain what's on offer. Skilled graphic design can set the tone for your sales pitch and provide your offering with a promotional personality. Undoubtedly one of the hallmarks of good design is that the outcome looks effortless. But be careful with DIY. Simply having a computer will not make you a designer any more than having a drill will make you a dentist.

Companies that invest in design outperform those who do not.

- According to a British Design Council survey, companies that invest in design outperform those who do not. So there is a likely **return on investment**. If one of the main aims of graphic design is to enable clear communication (and it is), then it makes sense to assume that those organisations that communicate better than their competitors will be providing themselves with a distinct advantage.

What really matters is whose widget is presented most effectively.

- Some organisations remain hesitant in investing in professional design support, preferring instead to utilise unskilled internal resources. Others reject design completely and rely on what they see as the superiority of their product or service to persuade would-be customers. Both angles could be a mistake if competitors produce **more seductive marketing material**. In reality, it doesn't actually matter if your widget is better than theirs. What really matters is whose widget is presented to the customer most effectively.

- Skilful graphic design can help set your organisation apart and help you present your offering more impressively than your competitors'. If done well it can, in an instant, convey quality, value, age, youth, complexity, simplicity or almost any other attribute you would want to be associated with your product or service. This means that your target audience **can evaluate the offering quickly** and make those all important buying decisions. Anything that can achieve all this in split seconds should be taken seriously.

- **Clear communication** sits at the heart of sales and organisational success. The list of potential items that can carry useful messages is almost endless – business cards, stationery, websites, brochures, flyers, folders, leaflets, newsletters, presentation slides, mailers, labels, packaging, display and exhibition stands, information packs, product sheets, posters, billboards – and all the web-based equivalents such as blogs and e-flyers. Graphic design is the tool that will help you to make optimum use of these opportunities to communicate.

- Many graphic designers move effortlessly across the divide between print and online media. However, there are important differences in the way both mediums function and consequently how they should be tackled in design terms. When hiring a designer do check that their skills suit your needs. Genuinely talented graphic designers are passionate to the core. Invariably their career chose them rather than the other way around. Seek out those with a **relevant qualification or else a proven track record**. Don't hesitate to shop around and do look for simplifiers not complicators. Rapport is as important as creative skill.

> **Shop around and look for simplifiers not complicators.**

- Graphic design is not about personal whim. It should not be about what the designer happens to like – nor for that matter should it be about what the client likes either. It is an **objective management process** that can help you meet defined and realistic aims. Therefore good design is not a matter of opinion but that which effectively achieves the required result.

- It is wise to have some idea of your required outcome before seeking a provider. The best way to ascertain if the explosively coiffured, bolt-nosed, heavy on the body art, mumbling goth is the right person to create your clinically precise annual report is to ask to see examples of previous work. Graphic design can be a horses-for-courses commodity. Attributes to look for include professionalism, knowledge of type and of colour, artistic skills, literacy and competency with current design software packages and reproduction techniques. It will help if your provider is imaginative, open-minded, co-operative and creative too – but never expect them to be good at spelling!

- Chartered designer and expert Andy Griib advises that most local trade directories and associations can help you **find a graphic designer** as will the Chartered Institute of Designers. Alternatively, look for work you admire and find out who did it. Before commissioning design work confirm who will own the intellectual property rights to the finished work and establish, in writing, if there will be any restrictions to your use of it. Some practitioners carry professional indemnity insurance for the reassurance of their clients.
- When briefing graphic design, start with the objective and work outwards towards the optional possibilities. For example, 'I want to send information on XYZ product to 1,000 industry decision-makers. I want to excite them and I want to prompt them to find out more'. **Outlining your aim** is enough. Try to stop short of telling the designer exactly what to do or how to do it.
- It will benefit both parties if the design project is broken down into stages or progress milestones, with each stage being signed off before the next proceeds. This approach will help **control the process** and prevent unexpected surprises. Expect (or request) that each stage be specified, pre-quoted and time-scaled in writing. Hold regular updates and keep communication lines open.

Control the process and prevent unexpected surprises.

Summary

Clear communication is an investment – not a cost. Good graphic design is a strategic management discipline, which can have a huge influence on the difference (and the distance) between success and failure. The DIY option is tempting but could be expensive in the long term. Graphic design can be vital in helping your organisation achieve a strong visual identity, and promote a powerful awareness of your offering, along with a familiarity and affinity between you and your customers. It can also be the key ingredient in setting you apart from your competitors. If your sales argument is more evident, more persuasive or just more likeable it will probably be more successful too.

Also read sections: 10; 20; 21; 45

23 Website design

Website design and graphic design may be similar but they are not the same. How they differ depends on who you listen to.

Depending on who you ask, there are at least three different priorities that can influence website design. Quiz a designer and you will likely find that his or her preferred emphasis is on look 'n' feel – with plenty of helpful blank space to separate the visual elements. A technically minded website builder, on the other hand, will be obsessively concerned with download speeds, redundant code and browser compatibility. Different still, a strategic marketer will be focused on the site's objectives, the target profile and the online promotional strategy. However, there is one aspect they probably all agree on: the need to look different from, and at least as good as, the competition – who, we should never forget, are only a few clicks away.

- Start by gathering the information that will influence your final plan. For example, what are your **marketing objectives**? How will your website realistically contribute to those objectives? Who and where are your targets? What will your website provide for visitors and how will they get to know about it? How much of the work can you do yourself? What specialist support might you need?

> **Set aside your own preferences and design the site to appeal to those you aim to attract.**

- Identify your **target markets** carefully and understand thoroughly what makes them tick. The more you can learn about their preferences the closer you will get to making a perfectly **tailored pitch**. Set aside your own likes and dislikes and design the site to appeal to those you aim to attract. Like all marketing tools, your website should be built around **purpose rather than personal preference.** Consider involving a 'useability' specialist.

> **You should think twice before deciding to DIY.**

- Visit your **competitors' websites**. Look at how they do things and see what ideas you can **adopt or adapt**. It can often be helpful to study a sample selection of design styles and ask a few trusted clients to comment. You can then form your own approach around some of the winning elements. Remember that the internet is a highly competitive arena – your website must compete adequately. For this reason alone you should think twice before deciding to DIY.

- Remember that you will need to **attract visitors** to your website. Consider your **promotional strategy** in advance, because the method or methods you adopt could influence the design process. Consider the site address. For commercial sites this will be more effective if it contains a description of what the site provides rather than who owns it. For example, www.bobsmotors.com usefully explains more than www.bobjohnson.com. When you have secured your **domain name** be sure to **display it on literature**, stationery, vehicles and anywhere else that potential visitors can see it.

- There are a variety of active ways to **promote your website**: Search engine optimisation; reciprocal links; affiliate schemes; and pay-per-click being among the most popular. What's important here is that the design of your site should support rather than obstruct your promotional opportunities. Having a **site map** will help search engines to evaluate your site. If you have sponsored pay-per-click links it is wise to have your visitors land directly at a sales page rather than the home page.

It is wise to have your visitors land directly at a sales page rather than the home page.

- Consider the technical capabilities and likely equipment of your intended audience. Avoid using **trendy tricks** that might prove awkward for visitors. When in doubt, keep it simple. Download speed is important – if the site fails to perform quickly and smoothly then it fails, full stop. Think carefully before using large or complex files, **animations**, auto-scrolling text or video unless you can be sure of fast, first-time performance. **The technology and features you adopt should not come between you and the viewer.**

- Some surfers switch off the image-viewing facility at their browser to improve download speed so don't hang all your expectations on **pictorial content**. This applies especially to using pictures or icons as navigation features. **Text-only navigation systems** are more reliable. Check your site's performance on **different browsers** to minimise incompatibility issues.

- **First impressions** count, so visual appeal is important. Too much information, poor layout, cumbersome or complex navigation, unclear prompts, inappropriate movement and over crowding are all best avoided. Also on the '**don't-do-it**' list are: **colours** that clash or vibrate; **pictures** that don't relate to the text; **type** that is too tightly line-spaced; and inconsistent page **layouts**. Research the styling of comparable websites to ensure that yours looks contemporary and compare useability.

'Marketing speak' is especially unpopular online.

- Headlines should be clear and specific, text should be succinct. Avoid the need to scroll where possible and bear in mind that speed-reading or scanning is a natural preference on the internet. Keep your tone-of-voice friendly – **talk with your reader** rather than at them. Avoid trite '**marketing speak**' which, according to research, is especially unpopular online. Do remember to **lead your reader** rather than risk letting them drift. Consider ending each section or each page with an **action prompt** or next-step link.
- Check your **legal obligations**. These might include: website terms and conditions, privacy policy (including data protection); sale terms and conditions (including distance selling regulations); and Disability Discrimination Act (visual access). You should also assert your intellectual property rights over design and content. When in doubt, seek qualified legal advice.
- Align your website design with your visual or **organisational identity**. Ensure that it is clear and understandable to visitors. Include a '**contact**' facility to enable readers to reach you with feedback or to ask a question. Warn if a download will be large, check regularly for broken links and **keep it interesting**!

Summary

Consider and fix the aims of the website before you do anything else. Plan to meet your marketing objectives. Also plan your promotional strategy before commencing the design or build. Design before build, not during. Design to appeal to your target audience. The build must support your promotional strategy and provide seamless technical performance. Avoid pointless trendy tricks and anything else that slows download speed. Use text navigation systems and keep all text content clear, legible and interesting. End pages or sections with an action prompt. Observe legal obligations. Ensure external specialist providers are adequately qualified in the relevant disciplines and agree fees and timescales in writing, in advance.

Also read sections: 6; 22; 27; 34; 44

24 Features, benefits, action

'The trio of temptation that tells us what it is, what it will do and what must be done to get it.'

In less strategically enlightened times advertisements often comprised solely of an interesting (though not always relevant) picture and the name of the product or business. For example, a tobacco ad from 1895 shows two horse-drawn fire appliances racing to a blaze. The words Planet and Neptune Tobaccos appear alongside. There is no evident link between words and picture and no proposal contained in the headline to suggest that the company or its products are in any way special. By contrast, another tobacco ad – this time from 1953 – shows a celebrity of the day smoking the product while urging, 'Ask yourself . . . do you have all this with your present cigarette? – clean, fresh taste after smoking, full enjoyment of food, freedom from cigarette cough, mouth and throat comfort, all day smoking enjoyment. If you answer 'No' to ANY of these questions – it's time to change to Philip Morris!' Product benefits and the call-to-action had arrived!

The call-to-action helps to turn a browser into a buyer.

- Marketers have learned that it is not sufficient to convey to a potential buyer of a product or service its name alone. It cannot be assumed that the buyer (or influencer) will work out why the purchase might be beneficial or how to see it through. The purchase decision must be primed by highlighting the salient gains that the buyer will experience and by leading the way towards a transaction. Features and benefits are the primers to many sales propositions. The call-to-action helps to ensure that a browser becomes a buyer.

- **Features** are the characteristics of a product or service – how it looks, how it works or how it is made. For example, 'This **award-winning, yellow** vacuum cleaner uses **new D120 technology** and is made from **hard-wearing components** which can be **easily replaced** if necessary.' The statement contains five features. Features specify what a product or service IS.

- **Benefits** tell the buyer what the product or service DOES for them. Not the technical role it fulfils, or the methods it uses, but what it will do to enhance their life, their experience or in meeting their emotional needs. This is important because purchase decisions are generated by emotion (benefits) and then justified by logic (features). Therefore, any sales pitch that targets emotional needs will be more effective. For example, an ad for a snoring cure could say, 'Buy this neat snoring cure' – but that option offers no real benefit. Alternatively, the ad could say, 'Save your marriage – stop snoring' – and immediately achieve more impact.

Purchase decisions are first prompted by emotion then justified by logic.

- It is widely assumed that **benefits should precede features** to attract customer interest. Generally this is so but there **are notable exceptions**. When the target market is composed of experts, enthusiasts, or specifiers, the features (performance, components, compatibility, colour, size, technical data) may be of more interest than regular benefits. Passionate hi-fi enthusiasts, for example, will be more impressed with technical performance than by colour, convenience or cost. The use of breakout panels to highlight technical data can be an advantage here.

- Wise marketers turn features (what it IS) into emotional benefits (what it DOES). You can do this for yourself by using '**which means that** . . .' against each feature. For example, this vacuum cleaner has won an award, **which means that** . . . it is probably very special, **which means that** . . . it passed all the tests and is reliable, **which means that** . . . I am reassured, my partner will be pleased that I've spent wisely and my neighbours will be envious. Keep applying the 'which means that' filter until the process reaches bottom – where you will find the real benefit that convinces the buyer.

- **Outstanding benefits** can sometimes be elevated beyond sales prompts and become a **Unique Selling Proposition (USP)** for the business as a whole. This is especially useful where the benefit would provide a unique accolade that would help set the organisation apart from its competitors. For example, the award-winning vacuum cleaner company could promote itself as 'Daring to be different' or 'Creating envy – worldwide'. To summarise: feature – what it IS; benefit – what it DOES; USP – how we are different.

- People buy benefits, not biographies. Features and benefits should be built around the interests of the buyer, not the history of the seller. **Relevance is vital**, as is the appreciation that one size will not

People buy benefits, not biographies.

fit all. Different markets will have different characteristics that will require a different sales pitch.

- Features and benefits are two key ingredients of any sales communication. The third key ingredient is **the call-to-action**. The aim of this is to lead the reader from interest in the offering to the threshold of acquiring it. Common examples include: click here to talk to an advisor; buy at this special offer price today and get £x off; free parking for the first 20 applicants; act now while stocks last. The call-to-action should be simple, authoritative and clear. It should also contain a hint of urgency and, where apt, the implied risk that failure to act could result in disappointment.

It should contain a hint of urgency and the implied risk that failure to act could result in disappointment.

- Features, benefits and calls-to-action frequently entail making a claim or an offer. Tread carefully, making false claims or misleading offers is a legal offence. Check your legal position – consult the Trade Descriptions Act or the Advertising Standards Authority.

Summary

Features explain what the offering IS, benefits highlight what it DOES. Benefits highlight the gains that connect with the buyer's emotional needs. Emotional needs are stronger buying prompts than logical needs. Features can be distilled into benefits by repeatedly applying 'which means that . . .' until the real benefit is identified. Outstanding benefits can be turned into an organisational USP, which can in turn differentiate the organisation from others. Advantageous pricing can be treated as a benefit. Generally, benefits are placed more prominently than features, except when communicating with those who find the features and specification information to be more interesting. The call-to-action prompts the reader to make or confirm a purchase.

Also read sections: 9; 20; 26; 37; 42

CHAPTER FIVE

Making the best use of the (well) written word

In this chapter:

25. **Writing business letters** – don't underestimate the snail-mail option
26. **Headline news** – get the headline right and the rest is easy
27. **Wise web-words** – writing for the internet and other digital declarations

25 Writing business letters

Dear Sir or Madam. Don't underestimate the snail-mail option – the person-to-person letter is still an effective marketing tool.

Having a bank account or a business involvement is enough to ensure that you receive plenty of propositional mail, much of which will probably trouble your attention for just a few moments prior to being disposed of. Many such letters fail because they repeat common mistakes – being gushing, insincere, arrogant, self-centred or plain unrealistic. Most fail simply because they attempt too much, often providing a first-time introduction then, seconds later, soliciting for a sale. But these less welcome traits obscure the potential of person-to-person business letters. Providing it is well produced, a good letter can put your name and your case directly into the hands of a key influencer. And, if you can achieve that for just a few pence, it has to be worth a try.

- **Before you start**, consider what you are trying to achieve and tailor accordingly. For example, if you merely wish to introduce yourself or establish contact (which you can build on later) make no proposals but do ask questions. If you aim to provide news, attach details and ask if a demonstration would be of interest. If you intend offering sales or services, include a personalised special offer or voucher. The point is to turn the letter into a prompt that encourages the recipient to respond or engage. Also consider presentation – always neat and uncluttered, not too busy – and timing. Avoid sending letters to arrive on Mondays when the recipient may be preoccupied or pressured, and Fridays for the same reason.

- **Use a headline** to focus the recipient on the topic. This need not be bigger than the main text but it can be bolder. Here's an example of one that worked for me – 'An invitation to the innovative marketer'. Here's one that didn't – 'We can give you the skills you need to succeed'. Can you see the difference? **The opening sentence** is also vitally important. It should continue the engagement begun by the headline and lead the reader into the main text. Here's one that won me over – 'This news could provide you with a business advantage'. Here's one that failed to draw me in – 'MBNB and African Express are pleased to invite you to apply for the . . .'. Opening with a short, interesting story that leads gently to the point of the letter is another useful technique.

- **Personal relevance** is a must. If your letter is not correctly addressed to, and personally relevant to the recipient your ambition could fall at the first hurdle. If the head of Rolls Royce cars can personally sign an annual customer letter to ALL customers (and he does) maybe that's a lesson for us all. Once you've got your first draft down, go through it and change 'I', 'me' and 'we' to 'you', 'you're' and 'your' to ensure that the letter talks TO the recipient rather than ABOUT the sender. If you can weave the recipient's company name into the benefits so much the better.

If your letter is not personally relevant to the recipient your ambition could fall at the first hurdle.

- **Put the key benefits near the top**, maybe under the first paragraph. Keep them short and punchy and emphasise them by an indent and a dash or bullet point. Main text should be credible, anything too fanciful will undermine the whole letter as with this example – 'You have caught our attention! Your loyalty as a faithful entrant is outstanding, and therefore you deserve to be . . .'. Given that I had been asking the sender to stop sending, perhaps this letter just didn't ring true.

- **Write to be understood.** Many non-professional writers revert to their schooldays when organising business letters. Instead of aiming to write conversationally, as though they are talking with a friend (a good habit), they become self-conscious and begin using those stiff, awkward terms favoured by English teachers (and law firms). If writing does not come naturally to you it might be better to look for support.

- **Form a conclusion.** Don't leave the recipient dangling, create a next step, such as: making a risk-free, timebound offer; asking a question; asking for an appointment; saying you'll call next Tuesday. The point is that each letter should be made to work like it's the only one you will ever send, not like it's one of millions that can be forgotten about.

Each letter should work like it's the only one you will ever send, not like it's one of millions.

- **The seven deadly sins.** Avoid the following: low quality data; scruffy presentation; impersonal salutation; poor spelling or grammar; irrelevant content; uncompelling content; a weak conclusion.

- **Winning checklist.** One way of ensuring that your letter is a winner, not a sinner, is to ask two or three (preferably uninvolved) colleagues to read it and give you an honest scorecard feedback against the following points: (1) Presentation – first impressions count. (2) Personalisation – person-to-person, not mass mailing. (3) Relevance – about the recipient and in their language. (4) Impact – the heading and first few lines resonate. (5) Benefits – quickly and clearly put. (6) Credibility – looks and talks like a quality communication. (7) Action – leading to a next step. (8) Final PS – delivers a 'killer' comment.

- **Tips.** Avoid poor quality personal data – compile your own list as an alternative. Avoid blanket salutations such as 'Dear Valued Customer'. Avoid messing up names – I get fed up with being addressed as 'Dear Mr Mura'. If the decision maker is too high up, write to their PA. Collect other sender's examples for study. Send a follow-up letter featuring happy customer testimonials. Write three different letters and test to see which works best.

Avoid blanket salutations such as 'Dear Valued Customer'.

Write three different letters and test to see which works best.

Summary

Consider what you aim to achieve and build your letter accordingly. Each intention requires a separate strategy. If your target is too remote write to the PA. Work hard on presentation. Use a headline that creates rapport or interest. Use good data to make sure you have full names and titles. Use a personal salutation rather than 'Dear Customer'. Use terms and content that are relevant to the recipient. Replace any references to you and your situation in favour of them and theirs. Put key benefits near the top. Be credible with tone and content. Write to be understood and use the winning checklist.

Also read sections: 21; 24; 26; 47

26 Headline news

'The job of the headline is to capture attention – get it right and the rest will be so much easier.'

T.S. Eliot helped us understand the value of a good headline when he astutely commented, '*If you start with a bang, you won't end with a whimper*'. Apparently, headlines are read 20 per cent more than text matter and those that promise a benefit have four times the hitting power when measured against those that merely introduce a product or service. Long headlines attract more attention than short, though this needs to be considered in context – direct doorstep mail and press ads provide the best opportunity for a long read because the reader is likely to be holding them while static. Media aimed at readers on the move, however, such as outdoor poster sites, must play a different game and usually favours shorter headlines – often combined with bigger pictures.

> **Marketing headlines don't provide an indexing service, they act as bait.**

- **News headlines and marketing headlines** are different. The role of a news headline is to summarise the main point of an article, but the article could be one of many on a page or screen, so the headline helps the reader to decide what to read and what to skip. Marketing-related headlines are aimed at attracting attention and enticing the reader to form a deeper interest – they don't provide an indexing service, they act as bait.

- **Impact and easy assimilation** are vital. Marketing headlines must be both noticeable (so design is important), and relevant (so some knowledge of the target reader's motives is essential). It will help readers to assess the headline's message if it is: concise; easy to read; near the top of the page or screen; framed by clear space; not set in capital letters or overrun with initial capitals for every word (only nouns).

- **Keep it lean**. This example headline ticks five boxes that could win customer interest, yet it is only nine words in length: 'Discover another way to save on your car insurance'. Analyse the job it does. 'Discover . . .' – so it's new to the reader; 'another way . . .' – so it's different from other offers; 'to save . . .' – so it's a good financial deal; 'on your . . .' – so it's pertinent to the reader; and finally 'car insurance . . .' – so the reader knows exactly what it's about. Look for other examples of lean headlines.

- **Appeal to the reader**, not the author or the marketer. To write 'Smiths to hold handbag clearance sale' focuses on the store and its own intentions. To write 'Handbag extravaganza – bargains galore!' brings the focus back to the customer and adds a benefit, but it might be too down-market for the store. To write 'Good news for bag ladies' is amusing but could confuse the point and risks offence. To write 'Quality handbags – unique sales event' makes the point with a hint of dignity. These examples demonstrate that there is often more than one way to proceed.

> To write 'Good news for bag ladies' could confuse the point.

- **Headlines in a list** are best treated factually both on and offline. For example, UN mission to study African wars, Fashion King dies at 71, Puerto Rico win buoys Clinton. Headlines written this way lend credibility and authority. They reveal enough about the context of the story to inform the reader, but avoid going into detail.
- **Promotional headlines** are more upbeat and usually contain a claim or make an offer to draw the reader in: 'The ultimate goose down duvet' or 'Refreshing summer offers in store now' or 'Loft ladders at unbeatable prices' or 'Big savings on gym equipment for your home'. This selection shows that promotional headlines get to the point quickly.
- **Advertising headlines** reveal a more subtle approach: 'Turns heads' or 'Imagine . . .' or 'Grooming Marvellous' or 'Take it to the edge'. These examples demonstrate how advertising can often be about conveying a brand image rather than a specific selling message. For example, the famous Wonderbra poster campaign of 1994 was voted tenth in a 'Poster of the Century' contest and was exhibited at London's Victoria and Albert Museum. Its headline was simply 'Hello Boys'.
- **Long headlines.** Having said that advertising often favours short headlines, there are always exceptions to every rule. Charles Saatchi adapted the text for a health education poster from an information pamphlet. The headline is 73 words long and begins 'This is what happens when a fly lands

> The headline is 73 words long and begins 'This is what happens when a fly lands on your food . . .'

on your food . . .', then goes on to graphically describe how flies feed before concluding with the sentence 'And then, when they've finished eating, it's your turn'.

. . . And when they've finished, it's your turn!

- **Words that work.** Useful headline techniques that can encourage readers to engage are: personal relevance – 'Now you can . . .' or 'Why you should . . .'; posing a question – 'isn't it time you took a break', or 'What would you say if . . .'; and offering knowledge – 'The secrets of sleep revealed' or 'How to sleep well'. The 'How to' route is particularly useful for its ability to appear in the many internet searches beginning with 'How to . . .'.

- **Tips.** You can imply authority or testimonial support by putting a headline in quotes – though you should not attempt to deceive of course. Never settle for the first headline you write. Always test on the uninitiated before making a final choice. Be very careful with sensational headlines and humour, both of which can backfire. Talk about the positive effects of your offering rather than the negative aspects of somebody else's. The golden rule: if you have to explain what a particular headline means, throw it away.

If you have to explain what a headline means, throw it away.

Summary

Tailor your headline to the needs or interests of the reader not the preferences of the writer or the ego of the marketer. Write to suit the chosen media – look to see what succeeds before you start. Consider whether your headline is about news or about gaining attention – what's your objective? A good headline will not survive bad presentation – no impact, no result. Refer to the easy assimilation checklist. Keep it lean and to the point. Never go with your first idea, always write at least six options and then get a guinea pig to give you feedback. Remember that the headline is the doorway to everything else – don't accept compromise.

Also read sections: 13; 24; 37; 42; 43

27 Wise web-words

Writing for the internet and other digital declarations requires a different approach if you want to avoid monitor myalgia.

The internet continues to define itself as the fastest growing, furthest reaching communication resource of all time. We have become accustomed to finding and absorbing information quickly. Inevitably, this is having an effect on how organisations must state their case. It is no longer adequate to rehash a brochure to fit online pages. We now know that our competitors are just a couple of clicks away and that we must sharpen our act if we are to compete adequately. In these circumstances it is quite possible that poor communication is actually worse than none at all. This section offers information and advice that will help you make best use of the worldwide megamedium.

Know what you want to achieve before you begin to write.

- As with writing for any other medium the first things to get straight are your **purpose and objectives**. Ask yourself: Why am I writing this? Who am I writing it for? What do they want to happen? What do I want to happen? How will the medium affect my intentions? Know what you want to achieve before you begin to write and keep your aims in front of you as you proceed. Keeping your objective in view will help you into the habit of ending each page with a **call-to-action** – prompting your reader to commit to a natural next step.

- Consider the **needs of the reader** and make your text relevant to them (rather than you). Be interesting, be specific, be clear; be polite, be friendly. Use language and expressions that your readers use. Avoid jargon and elitisms. Rather than talk *at* your reader, talk *with* them. Conversational writing is not only more friendly but also more effective in winning the confidence of readers.

Only 16 per cent of us read web pages word by word while 79 per cent scan.

- Not all communication mediums work the same way. Reading from a monitor is about 25 per cent slower than reading from paper. Most web readers **scan** rather than read detail. According to research carried out by Jakob Nielsen, one of the world's most eminent experts on website usability, only 16 per cent of us read web pages word by word while 79 per cent scan.

Scrolling pages are also a turn-off. The most obvious remedy is simply to write less text. Nielsen suggests that 50 per cent less text, compared with paper documents, is about right.

- As web use becomes more commonplace surfers are becoming quicker at making decisions about a site. Research suggests that the click-away time can be as fast as half a second – so clear headlines have become very important, both in the way they are written and how they are displayed. Headlines that pack a punch or contain a benefit or promise will encourage further reading. Don't settle on a headline until you have tested it (or several) on an uninitiated guinea pig and don't ruin its potential by surrounding it with distracting animation.

- The writing style is important throughout the main text too. Naturally, your message will need to be organised and sequentially planned so that it makes sense. Write in short sentences and be concise. The internet tends to be used as a quick information medium, not as an opportunity for a long and leisurely read. So succinct text works better than droning descriptions. For example, 'This screedpump is the market leader' rather than 'Our development team worked long and hard to come up with a screedpump design that fully meets the needs of . . .'.

Succinct text works better than droning descriptions.

- Clear layout and sensible use of type are essential. Use simple font styles and avoid mixing more than **two font families**. The more you chop and change the more optical adjustments your reader will have to make. This could affect their attention. **Allow plenty of clear space** around each chunk of text and use occasional subheads or 'pull quotes' to break up long passages. Avoid using typefaces or fonts that are not commonly available on most computers. Computers can only display the fonts they have installed and will otherwise default to what could be an ugly or unhelpful substitute.

- Put the most relevant and enticing text at the **beginning of paragraphs** and try to avoid having more than two consecutive paragraphs without a change of visual tempo or a clear-space break. To assist the skim-reading process you can **embolden key phrases** but don't overdo it. Ballpoints or bullet points can be very effective on web pages and are helpful in cutting down long-winded explanations – remember, less is more.

- Website visitors will respond positively to a warm and welcoming personality just the same as real-world shoppers. The difference is that demonstrating a personable smile or a friendly welcome is harder on a website than it would be in person. But this is not insurmountable. By knowing that it could be a problem, you are halfway towards resolving it.

Visitors respond positively to a warm welcoming personality just the same as real-world shoppers.

- Rather than interrupt the flow of text to explain a side issue it can be helpful to refer to it briefly, then add a **hyperlink** to the full story for anyone who wants the detail. This technique also helps to reduce the risk of excessively large text slabs and excessive scrolling pages.
- A final word on dates and updating. Unlike paper-based information that eventually tends to get taken down, blown away or screwed-up, web information stays exactly the same – forever. So be careful not to imply that your entire site is out of date by leaving old and expired date references strewn around. Search engines favour websites that are refreshed or updated regularly. Keep your written content up to date.

Summary

Get your objectives straight and refer to them regularly as you write. Identify the readers you are targeting and keep your content relevant to them. Take care to use clear language and terms, avoid jargon. Be interesting – write conversationally but have something worthwhile to say. Keep it short and concise. Long rambling sentences do not help. Bear in mind that most readers do not read at all, they scan. Help readers with good headlines and selectively emboldened phrases. Organise your text so that the reader is drawn from one step to the next. Avoid overloading pages and scrolling text. Check the legal requirements on word legibility.

Also read sections: 13; 23; 26; 33

CHAPTER SIX

Popular marketing media and options

In this chapter:

28. **All the world's a stage** – selecting the right communication options
29. **Advertising** – what it is and where it works best
30. **Direct marketing** – the benefits of getting up close and personal
31. **Effective PR** – accentuate the positive, eliminate the negative
32. **Trade shows and exhibitions** – the boredom, the foot-powder and the glory
33. **Internet options** – from blooming blogs to steady streaming
34. **Internet marketing** – a whole not-so-new world of shopportunity
35. **In-house marketing** – ihm = diy = roi = happy accountants
36. **Telemarketing** – turning cold contacts into hot prospects
37. **Sales promotion** – exclusive special offer, read now while stocks last!
38. **Word-of-mouth marketing** – creating envoys and ambassadors
39. **Mobile marketing** – moving with the market

28 All the world's a stage

> *Contact and productive communication with your customers is vital – selecting the most appropriate way to go about it is pretty important too.*

Customers at my father's shop would spend an inordinate amount of time studying the tantalising confectionery. They would make a circuit, examining jars, bars and packets then, just when you thought they'd made a decision, they'd flit back to the chocolate counter and start again. Often, after several indecisive minutes these perplexed punters would suddenly make a choice, lunging for their prize with one hand, while simultaneously paying with the other, as though they knew that matters should be completed before doubt set in. Frequently, the item they chose would be the same thing they always chose, suggesting that too many options can be immobilising, causing us to stick with what we know best. In the context of marketing this is not good.

The key disciplines are advertising, public relations, sales promotion, direct marketing and personal selling.

- The methods used by organisations to communicate with their customers are sometimes referred to as the **promotional mix**. 'Promotional' because promoting the business and its offerings is the aim. 'Mix' because it is best to adopt a blend of methods rather than relying on just one. The key promotional mix disciplines are advertising, public relations, sales promotion, direct marketing and personal selling. However, this list rather oversimplifies the number of options available.

- More specifically, communication options include: **advertising** – local and national press, posters, directories, radio, TV, internet and other mass media; **public relations** – publicity, press management, media relations; **sales promotion** – point-of-sale displays, special offers, special schemes; **direct marketing** – direct mail and email, telemarketing, mobile phone messaging; **personal selling** – sales team, telesales, sampling, networking. As if that's not enough to consider, you can also add: **the internet** – websites, email, blogs, podcasts and social networking sites; **event marketing** – exhibitions, trade shows, sponsored events; **influencer marketing** – referrals, advocate schemes, viral programmes . . . By now I'm sure you get the idea. There are plenty of options – so how do you find the best?

Answering the seven following questions will help you to decide on the best methods of reaching your customers.

Either you want to raise your profile, or you want to create sales.

- **What is your objective?** Broadly speaking there are two options here – either you want to raise your profile, create and extend awareness of your organisation, or you want to create sales. Raising profile is usually a matter of using a scattergun approach to keep your name, colours, logo, brand message in view. Making sales, however, calls for putting a specific message (buy this, pay that) in front of a decider or an influencer.

- **Who are you trying to reach?** This question must be answered specifically. The options include: trade or consumer targets; local, regional, national or international targets; wealthy or poor; old or young; male or female and so on. It doesn't matter if this profiling exercise fails to identify a one word answer, as long as you avoid a ten word answer. Each different target mindset requires a tailored approach.

- **Where do they look?** Rather than guess, find out exactly where your customers look and what they respond to. You can waste huge amounts of money and effort by failing to put your communication in the optimum place. For example, discovering that buyers of your engineering products will accept emailed product updates from you will save money and put you in direct contact with a decider. Similarly, advertising your sports injury clinic in a gym or rugby club is likely to be more productive than a video clip on Facebook. It's a case of courses for horses.

- **What do your competitors do?** Never ignore your competitors. Always observe their activity when forming your own plans. Look at how and where they promote themselves because there might be clues for you. Look at what they say and how they say it, look at the language they use and the claims or offers they make. Get a picture of how they do business. The more you know about them the easier it will be to avoid them or outshine them.

- **What can you afford to do?** This question must be answered specifically, firstly because your plans should have an identified budget and secondly because you can't spend what you don't have. So planning a TV campaign to promote your expensive, state-of-the-art e-commerce website will be a completely unrealistic ambition for most organisations. Always set realistic budgets but don't be intimidated by their modest size (if this is the case). Small budgets are helpful because they force you to be more selective and more creative.

- **Should you compete or be different?** In some circumstances you will not be able to avoid direct competition. But, where you can avoid it you should. If you attempt to do the same as your competition, both sides will end up trying to outperform (and outspend) each other. You will be better off finding and amplifying your unique points of difference and playing to your strengths. Where possible avoid promoting alongside the enemy, but if you've no choice, invest in a more creative approach rather than a bigger, louder one.

You will be better off amplifying your unique points of difference and playing to your strengths,

- **Can you limit the risk?** All promotional communication is a risk even though many organisations seem to deny the fact. Risk itself is an undeniable truth of any competitive undertaking. But – and it's an important but – you can significantly limit risk in communicating with your customers simply by testing your approach and ideas beforehand. Never embark on an expensive exercise until you have first tested it on a relevant sample group.

You can significantly limit risk by testing your approach and ideas beforehand.

Summary

This is not the place for prescriptive recommendations – the best way to decide how you should communicate the attributes of your organisation is by reducing the options and making choices based on key questions. The promotional mix you adopt should be considered – not random or accidental. Identify clear objectives and know your targets. Know what they look at or respond to. Know what your competitors do and try to avoid them. If you can't avoid them then be different. Set a budget and avoid blowing it on promoting against the enemy rather than to the customer. Reduce promotional risk by spreading the message across different methods and by testing effectiveness first.

Also read sections: 9; 10; 12; 13; 18

29 Advertising

'The trade of Advertising is now so near to perfection that it is not easy to propose any improvement' *Samuel Johnson (1709–84)*

Global accounting experts PricewaterhouseCoopers have projected that worldwide advertisement spending will exceed half-a-trillion dollars by 2010. That's a lot of dollars, especially for an industry whose effectiveness has occasionally been challenged. But we shouldn't forget that advertising has always managed to survive its critics, one of whom was US department store pioneer John Wanamaker. He who famously complained, '*Half the money I spend on advertising is wasted; the trouble is, I don't know which half.*' The fact that Wanamaker hired the world's first in-house copywriter and paid him generously perhaps reveals his true opinion. Essentially a creative industry, advertising has continuously adapted itself to new challenges. There can be little doubt that the internet age will provide some very interesting challenges and possibilities.

- Definitions of advertising vary from simplistic – *the way sellers make themselves or their wares known* – to complicated – *planned, decisive and paid-for public exposure of a product or an organisation, aimed at raising awareness or prompting interest.* So, advertising tells people that you're around and whets their appetite. Curiously enough, advertising is not directly a sales vehicle as is commonly supposed.

- Advertising meets a number of roles. It can **inform**, by conveying news of your organisation and its offering. It can also **influence**, by introducing new ideas that drive trends or create desires. Advertising can also **promote** brand familiarity and loyalty. Advertising can set you apart or **differentiate** you from your competitors and it can be used to **persuade** a target audience to respond in a specific way. Advertising can also be used to **develop** an organisation, for example, by assisting in the recruitment process.

- Although there are known ancient examples of political advertising, the first recognisable advertisements appeared in 18th-century English newspapers. Initially, these Ads promoted books and medicines but the activity became progressively more generalised. In 1841, Volney Palmer established the first true advertising agency in Boston, USA. This was followed in 1875 by the first full-service agency – N.W. Ayer – in Philadelphia. The practice of advertising soon became established.

By the 1920s, it began to exploit the opportunity provided by commercial radio. There was no turning back – by the late 1940s and early 1950s the doors of mass appeal were fully opened by television.

- The 1950s and 1960s were the golden years of advertising. Mass media – press, TV and cinema – created mass markets. Efficient manufacturing delivered goods to homes where disposable incomes generated keen interest in product innovation. Two advertising forms evolved: brand advertising, which builds awareness and direct response advertising, which prompts action. The problem with brand advertising is that its effect on sales can be difficult to measure. Consequently, it provides limited value, especially as most advertisers prefer quantifiable results.
- Your advertising strategy should serve the overarching aims of your marketing strategy. The nature of your organisation and of the business you are in will define who your customers are and, therefore, whether you should advertise to business (B2B) or to consumers. In some circumstances it will be beneficial to do both. For example, a food manufacturer might advertise a new line in the trade press to influence supermarket interest (push strategy) whilst also advertising to consumers to create demand at the other end of the buying chain (pull strategy).

Your advertising strategy should serve the overarching aims of your marketing strategy.

- The medium you select (media strategy) for your advertising will be dictated by two things: its ability to reach your target audience and your ability to afford it. The options include: TV; the internet; radio; newspapers; trade journals; consumer and enthusiast press; outdoor media (poster sites); buses; trains and ambient media. Less mainstream options include: mobile phones; washroom media; airborne media and body media.

The medium you select will be dictated by its ability to reach your target audience and your ability to afford it.

- The first step in planning an Ad campaign is to define your objectives and your target audience – who are they? where are they? what do you want to say? what do they want to hear? what do you want them to do? how will you know if they did it? Timing too can be an issue. Consider when a breaking campaign might work in your favour or against you – are there other events

The first step is to define your objectives and your target.

planned for the same time (World Cup, Olympics, Christmas . . .) that could distract your target audience? Lead times for booking space can be longer than expected – check first. Timing for Ad placement in some directories can also be important. For example, you want your Ad in place ready for Christmas or the directory itself is only printed once a year, so missing the deadline could be a disaster. If you are planning to place an avalanche of successive press Ads – beware – this kind of operation can be complex. It might be wise to seek professional support.

- The classic **advertising planning process** goes like this: (1) **marketing strategy** – research and segmentation, positioning, branding; (2) **advertising strategy** – targets, media, budget planned and confirmed. Benchmarks set; (3) **campaign development** – creative angles, AIDA (see page 44 for further explanation); (4) **testing** – appeal and response; (5) **final development** – refinement and production; (6) **campaign launch** – deploy and maintain; (7) **evaluation** – analysis, benchmark comparison. This process can be adapted to individual needs.

- A study by researchers, TNS Media Intelligence, suggests that UK promoters are lagging behind their international counterparts in exploiting social media such as blogs and podcasts. According to the report, just 25 per cent of UK marketers believe that viral campaigns have real impact while 75 per cent of US respondents are convinced they do. Whether the potential of the internet as an advertising medium represents a fundamental shift or a temporary blip remains to be seen.

> **Just 25 per cent of UK marketers believe viral campaigns have impact while 75 per cent of US respondents are convinced they do.**

Summary

Advertising doesn't necessarily exist to make direct sales but it does sow the seeds of awareness and desire. Clear objectives should be identified, as should specific targets. Mass markets are a thing of the past (though the internet could change that). A diverse spread of media is a safer bet – budget permitting – but remember that each media option (press, TV, poster, etc) has distinct pros and cons, which should be considered. People are inclined to forget more than they remember so 'one-offs' are not a wise investment. Professional standards are defined and controlled by the ASA *www.asa.org.uk*.

Also read sections: 11; 26; 28; 33; 43

30 Direct marketing

‘Whether it's through your letterbox, onto your desktop or into your pocket, direct marketing is delivering a powerful message for the future.’

We (wife and self) recently booked a UK internal flight online – found the deal, filled out the application, clicked submit, job done. In no time the airline joined up the dots and emailed hire car info for our destination airport, which was very useful. Months later, they still send personalised special offers to tempt us. Does this trouble us or damage our view of their brand? No, not at all. The only thing that bothers me is why they have not yet sent promotional text messages – they have my mobile number (in case of flight delays apparently) – and part of me wants them to seize the opportunity to strut their stuff. Modern direct marketing has the potential to join the dots in so many different ways, the future could be an exciting place.

- Revered master marketer Drayton Bird **defined direct marketing** as '. . . *any advertising activity that creates and exploits a direct relationship between you and your prospect or customer* . . .' Its purpose is to create sales and raise awareness. The most obvious benefit of direct marketing is that it provides the seller with the opportunity to present their offering directly, in a one-to-one conversation with the buyer.

The benefit is that it provides the seller with a one-to-one conversation with the buyer.

- Direct marketing grew from the early success of direct mail. **The principle of direct contact** still applies but the ways in which prospects can be approached have moved beyond posted mail and now include email, telemarketing, database marketing, mobile telephone (SMS) messaging, interactive websites and interactive television – even radio and cinema. The potential of the internet and of mobile personal telephones have given the direct industry a new lease of life. Broadcast faxing and leaflet drops are now less popular following the arrival and development of more sophisticated methods.

There are three important constituents for a successful direct marketing campaign.

- Experts agree that the **three most important constituents** for a successful direct marketing campaign are: (1) the quality of the target list or database; (2) the quality of the offering – the product or service; (3) the quality of the communication – creativity, credibility and clarity. A deficiency in any of these aspects will affect the overall performance of the campaign.

- **Direct marketing scores** over other types of marketing because: targets can usually be prequalified; its direct-to-target nature reduces wasted resources; positive responses are measurable; it can be easily pretested; it can often be personalised to the recipient by name or circumstances; email, TV and SMS can reach high numbers of targets for comparatively low costs; it can often be timed to arrive with recipients at the right moment; it can be used in isolation or as part of a broader, integrated exercise.

- But it's not all plain sailing. Direct marketing does have a few **cautionary downsides**. While you can measure positive responses, you can't measure the possible negative effects of being seen as junk mail or spam. Lists or databases can be messy – the industry wastes tens of £millions each year by incorrectly targeting dead people. There are also legal issues to be observed (see the last bullet point in this section).

The industry wastes tens of £millions each year incorrectly targeting dead people.

- Experts stress the need for a good **target database** or list. One way to obtain a reliable database is to create your own. This should not simply be a list of names but should also contain useful details that will help you to categorise prospects. For example a holiday company would want to be able to separately target water-sport lovers or skiing enthusiasts. A high profile football club would want to send news and offers to their own fans' mobile phones. A ticket agency would want to offer theatre goers seats for exactly the right shows – perhaps musicals rather than drama or comedy.

- Alternatively, you can buy a **preformed database**. These come in two forms – compiled lists and response lists. Compiled lists are created using demographic, psychographic or geographic data collected from a variety of sources. Response lists feature targets known to have previously purchased a similar offering to yours, so they can be assumed to be interested in your genre. For example, if your prospect has previously bought a gardening book online their details could later appear on a list of gardening enthusiasts. Professional list brokers can be sourced through the Direct Marketing Association *www.dma.org.uk*.

- **Planning and costing** should happen before the campaign begins not once it is underway. Start by defining exactly what you intend to achieve. The cost of the campaign should preferably be covered by the results it creates. Your budget will include the cost of preparing or buying-in target lists plus as many of the following as appropriate: copywriting; design; HTML build; artwork; printing; postage costs; response processing and so on. Plan to test wherever possible and use your test responses to forecast the expected campaign results.

- **Ideas and tips.** Known past purchasers tend to buy again within the same category, so target them as a priority. Incentivised responses are more effective. 'Next purchase' discounts are also effective. Include yourself in the contacts database to check campaign efficiency and to get a feel for the target's experience. Make the most of your direct opportunity by personalising your approach as much as possible. A step-by-step guide to direct mail is available from the Royal Mail website *www.royalmail.com*. In-company training and advice can be found at *www.theidm.com*.

Incentivised responses are more effective.

- The way you manage and use information about your customers or potential customers, including how you contact them, is regulated by law. You can check your legal responsibilities for email marketing and data protection at *www.informationcommissioner.gov.uk*. You can check your responsibilities for telephone, mailing, email and fax preference service at *www.dma.org.uk*.

Summary

Direct marketing is activity targeted directly at an individual recipient. Common methods include email, telemarketing, database marketing, SMS (text), interactive websites and TV. Three aspects are crucial for success: the quality of the target list; of the offering and of the communication. Direct marketing is less wasteful than broadcast campaigns. Personalised marketing works particularly well. Bought-in lists may need 'cleaning'. Homemade lists should be segmented for best results. Always test a campaign before deploying it fully. Plan and budget your activity before implementing it. Check your legal responsibilities before proceeding.

Also read sections: 3; 24; 26; 28; 39

31 Effective PR

"You've got to accentuate the positive, eliminate the negative, latch onto the affirmative." Was Bing Crosby singing about the PR business?

According to the Centre of Economic and Business Research the PR industry employs 48,000 people in the UK, of whom 3,200 are apparently government press officers. The industry generates a respectable turnover of over £6 billion p.a., which gives a strong clue as to the importance of projecting (or protecting) reputations. Perceptions will inevitably shape opinions. Shaping and polishing the perceptions is what the PR business is about. Ultimately, PR is concerned with reputation – either by helping build a favourable one or by minimising the damage when something goes wrong. Some experts suggest that information placed by PR and published as editorial content can be between three and five times more effective than if the same space were used by conventional advertising. Good 'spin' indeed!

- PR, or public relations, is about managing communication. In practice, it's about getting people to talk or think about you (or your business or organisation) in a positive way – to see the best side of you, thus enhancing your reputation. PR does this, not by blatant advertising or promotion, but by influencing the established news media. Most commonly this can be achieved by spreading favourable news or by **emphasising the positive aspects** of an organisation or its products.

- PR can be used strategically to influence or change perceptions, delivering to predetermined objectives. Or it can be deployed tactically in response to developments, for example as a **crisis management tool**. The standard methods employed include: press relations and news releases; press briefing packs; newswire distribution; product placement and launches; podcasts and other internet news-feed links. PR practitioners frequently provide journalists with the information with which to build a story.

- Probably the key benefit of PR is that it puts news or information into believable context. Readers of editorial coverage or viewers of a news programme tend to assume that what they see or hear is accurate and impartial – and therefore credible. Whereas viewers of paid advertising will know

> **Readers of editorial coverage assume that what they see is accurate and impartial.**

that they are being fed biased information and might, therefore, resist it.

- PR can be targeted at a specific audience. This is done firstly by identifying the target group, then identifying the media most likely to reach that group and finally by ensuring that the news released is relevant to both. If news is to be sent to a variety of media contacts it is wise to adapt the first paragraph to appeal to the special interests of each contact if possible.

- PR, and those who provide it, can work at different levels from the local high street to the upper extremes of global communication. Some smaller practices are highly focused on specialised niche areas, for example, cosmetics or household goods. Others might specialise in broadcast PR or industrial labour relations. However, expert Graham Lowing of Wordsworth PR advises that a provider with a spread of clients shows versatility and flexibility. A skilled PR writer will rapidly assimilate the complexities of any client organisation.

A skilled PR writer will rapidly assimilate the complexities of any organisation.

- An example of PR in action: a manufacturer of motorised window openers became the sole UK stockist of high quality Italian components. This provided five PR opportunities. Firstly, the news was released to the trade press at a champagne reception held during a trade exhibition. Secondly, the news was celebrated in the staff newsletter and then featured in the local press because of its potential to support employment opportunities. The firm's existing customers each received a personal letter informing them of the announcement and finally the news was uploaded to the company's online news archive to be available to website visitors. One piece of news – five very different ways of using it.

One piece of news – five very different ways of using it.

- Arguably the most common PR tool is **the press release**. Lowing reminds us that a press release must be interesting enough and well written enough to appeal to the journalist first. Reporters, news editors and editors are the gatekeepers of a publication. If they don't like it, they won't print it. Make your first paragraph strong – cover the **who, what, when, where, why and how** details; keep it short and sharp; if the news is exciting let your enthusiasm come through. Aim to provide raw material that will support journalists: give them the makings of a good story; send samples or anything else that creates interest or attracts attention; submit interesting pictures but be subtle with background branding and remember to name those featured; include your contact details and be available for questions. Proofread and spell check – twice.

- A few cautions: send submissions to the editorial team only; don't agonise over the perfect headline, that's the sub-editor's job; avoid waffling on about your organisation's history or past achievements – unless they are specifically relevant; aim to complete the entire press release in two pages or less; avoid periods of major news or distractions that could make your story insignificant; stick to the facts and avoid exaggerated claims; avoid jargon, sales-speak and acronyms; don't bury the good or interesting news at the end, put it at the beginning; never assume that anything can be said confidentially 'off-the-record'; don't send so many pictures that you jam the system; avoid photographs of people wearing sunglasses.

Never assume that anything can be said confidentially 'off-the-record'.

- Despite occasional bad press (irony), most PR professionals are reputable practitioners. Those who are members of the Chartered Institute of Public Relations will have signed the CIPR Code of Conduct. The CIPR provides an online 'match-maker' service for those seeking to appoint a practitioner. Visit *www.cipr.co.uk*. Beware publishing statements that are untrue, defamatory or harmful amount to libel.

Summary

PR is the process of managing the supply and interpretation of information so as to enhance the reputation of an individual or an organisation. It is not predominantly about 'spin' or dirty tricks. PR can be deployed strategically, systematically or in a crisis. When it works well PR can be more powerful than advertising and is less expensive. When dealing with reporters or commentators never assume that anything can be said 'off-the-record'. It is better to be positive about your stuff than negative about competitor's stuff. Be aware of the libel laws – and don't ever be rude about the press.

Also read sections: 9; 13; 19; 21; 46

32 Trade shows and exhibitions

'Thinking beyond aching feet, trade shows provide an exciting opportunity to meet your peers, next year's trends and maybe next year's customers too.'

There are nearly 1,000 UK trade shows each year – 160 in the next two months according to exhibitions.co.uk. Buyers attending these events generally do so for four reasons: to recharge their batteries on where the industry is heading; to meet new customers or suppliers; to check their own situation within the industry and to spend undisturbed time with colleagues and peers away from the workplace. Some will also want to see live product or equipment demonstrations. The concentrated timescales make planning simple and minimise lost productivity. Online matchmaking enhances the networking potential and digitally managed booking, badging and data-capture make the process easier than ever before.

- **Trade shows and exhibitions** provide a rare opportunity to come face-to-face with buyers, specifiers and influencers in a neutral environment. As an added bonus, show visitors will be from a specific commercial sector, which means many of your important targets will be present. They too will be focused on making new contacts and renewing old ones so the networking potential is excellent. If you get it right, you can achieve more in three or four days at a trade show than in months of regular marketing activity.

- **Strategy** has an important part to play. Identify realistic objectives – successful exhibitors are those who know in advance what they need to do and exactly how they will do it. The design of your stand should also take account of your objectives. For example, those with a bulky product range might be better off showing looped video rather than cram the stand. Alternatively, those with one highly innovative product should display it for buyers to see and touch for themselves – don't forget to invite the trade press to come and do the same.

- Trade shows provide **three phases of opportunity** – before, during and after – each requires a separate approach. Pre-event activity could include contacting other exhibitors or inviting known contacts to visit your stand, try to arrange this for a specific time slot such as morning coffee or end-of-day cocktails.

Trade shows provide three phases of opportunity.

During the event you should be meeting people, demonstrating your wares and gathering as many contact names as possible. Make future appointments with as many as you can there and then. After the event hold a team debrief to record what worked well or otherwise. Aim to make all follow-up contacts within the week after the event.

Second-hand stand displays and accessories can be sourced from eBay.

- When **planning your stand** consider your location within the hall. Weigh up the options – shell scheme, space-only site, island or corner site. Avoid isolated corners or obscuring columns. Aim to be near bars, the entrance or the toilets where footfall is greatest. Health and safety has become a big issue in recent years so hiring expert exhibition stand contractors, who know the ropes, could be a wise investment. Begin planning earlier than you think necessary. Second-hand stand displays and accessories can be sourced from eBay.

- When calculating the **possible cost** of exhibiting include: your space, plus the cost of amenities such as power or water; design and construction of your stand; construction or hire of additional display equipment such as display screens or cases; the cost of promotional materials – leaflets or brochures – and event-related changes made to your website; staff and temp expenses – uniforms, food, hotel and travel, plus the cost of transporting equipment and products to and fro.

Your stand is your shop window – it must impress.

- **Manage your team**: for some, the excitement of a big event can lead to distraction and temptation. Make it clear that there is a job to be done and give each team member target tasks. Some experts suggest you should double the number of staff you think you'll need. Insist they take frequent breaks – providing they remain sharp and focused when on duty. Discourage eating on the stand unless it is part of your customer hospitality. Don't feel obliged to use your regular staff, especially if their appearance is not in line with your company image. You can easily hire and train agency temps, some of whom will be actors whose apparent warmth and enthusiasm can be priceless. Remember your stand is your shop window – it must impress.

- **Success tips**: moving images or interesting activity can attract attention; personnel or products at the front of the stand will act as a barrier; train staff to engage visitors with active, open questions;

impressive, co-ordinated livery can raise perceptions and emphasise your brand message – but don't squeeze an unwilling 22-stone beer monster into a figure-hugging sports top; have two levels of take-away information – cheapy leaflets for casual enquiries and a secret stash of expensive brochures for more serious visitors; don't blow all your sales support materials in one go or on non-trade days; have your team visit a similar event a few weeks beforehand to get the feel of things.

Don't squeeze an unwilling 22-stone beer monster into a figure-hugging sports top.

- **Personal survival tips** include: drinking plenty of water; taking breaks, exercising by walking to the furthest loo; avoiding large, greasy lunchtime blowouts; avoiding alcohol; remaining alert – perhaps with competitive scoring amongst team members. Most importantly, look after your feet and wear comfortable shoes. Always have an emergency kit with basic tools, tape and velcro, glucose sweets and an aspirin product.

- Ensure that the event organiser provides **Fire Regulations** and **Health and Safety requirements** including height restrictions and wheelchair access. Helpful information can be found at *www.aeo.org.uk* and *www.businesslink.gov.uk.*

Summary

Trade shows and exhibitions are an excellent opportunity to meet buyers and to network with peers. Fix a budget based on experience or tentative supplier quotations. Book your space first then organise your stand. Develop a strategy that will help you meet your objectives – set objectives rather than merely turning up. Set tasks and targets for team members. If you're using the event to launch an innovative product or service, invite the trade press and your PR people. Divide the event into three phases – before, during and after. Create a plan of action for each phase. Include something on your stand that encourages people to stop and look. Keep staff fresh.

Also read sections: 4; 9; 14; 31; 37

33 Internet options

> *From email and e-commerce to blogging, podcasting and streaming – the online revolution has brought new vocabulary and new opportunities.*

The internet has revolutionised the way people work and play. It has simultaneously made the world into a smaller place and a bigger opportunity – and it has done so in a relatively compact space of time. As it has changed the communication landscape, the web has engendered both the potential for new prizes and the need for new cautions – new possibilities give rise to new opportunists, some of whom must be controlled by equally new restrictions. The challenge for internet marketers will be to rise above the increasing noise to win the attention of their audience. Despite its marginal downsides, the internet remains a phenomenal opportunity for those who correctly identify appropriate strategies. In this section we look at a few of the most familiar aspects.

There's a good chance that some of what follows here will be out of date before the ink dries.

- **The internet** is developing so fast that there's a good chance that at least some of what follows here will be out of date before the ink dries. Whichever aspect of the internet you choose to exploit, your ambitions will go further and be more productive if you first develop a realistic strategy that takes into account: your target customers' profile; your marketing aims; the available, proven technology and your budget.
- **Email** can be finitely targeted and tracked; sent instantaneously, to single or multiple recipients; it does not require paper, print or postage and it can be highly flexible in the way it is presented. Small campaigns can be managed in-house using standard PC equipment and software. However, this tempting simplicity has led to unacceptable levels of spam (junk email). Spam filter rejection has become a major issue for emailshots. Remedies include asking the recipient to add the sender's email address to their address book, preventing rejection. Alternatively, some senders display the shot as an online webpage and send recipients a link to it. Emma Healey of Epsilon Media advises that the motives for emailshots need to be clear at the outset and will shape the design and frequency of the campaign. Recipients must be from an opted-in database and senders must offer unsubscribe options.

- **Brochure websites** are the most common type of marketing or promotional sites found on the internet. They can provide visitors with details of what your organisation does and usually have a built-in 'contact us' feature which enables visitors to make enquiries. At the next level, websites become more responsive – collecting valuable visitor data, offering complementary downloads and proactively building the brand relationship online.

- **E-commerce websites** are fully functional online shops. They can display goods for sale, explain professional services, enable transactions and process payments. A bespoke e-commerce site can be expensive and complex. However, lower priced self-build options are available for those with moderate technical skills. The great attraction of e-commerce sites is their potential ability to perform around the globe and around the clock.

> The attraction of e-commerce sites is their ability to perform around the globe and around the clock.

- **Social media** or social networks are online spaces where like-minded communities gather to meet and chat. Familiar examples include Facebook, MySpace, Bebo and the business oriented LinkedIn. The key attraction from the users' point of view is that social media is not overtly influenced by corporate regulation and is seen as being owned and driven by its followers, unlike mainstream media. From a marketing perspective, interest lies in the fact that users of social media are self-defining market segments. Successful exploitation of this point has helped launch several music business careers that might otherwise have remained unsigned.

- **Blogs and Wikis** are another form of socially democratic community where users can have their say or co-operate without traditional constraints. Blogs began as personal online journals but are increasingly proving useful to marketers as a low-friction means of communication and PR. A Wiki is an online resource that enables diverse contributors to edit, write and save the same document, the most famous example being Wikipedia. Wikis are rarely used overtly for marketing.

- **Podcasts and video streaming** have brought audio and video to the internet. As an example, internationally-based corporate managers could see and hear the key points of a management convention held in the UK without having to leave their desks. Inevitably, video media such as YouTube will affect consumer expectations, leaving traditional static media looking dated. Marketers will be viewing developments with interest.

- **Search engines** still represent the largest potential source of traffic for any website. While results may not be instant, any effort invested in making your website rank highly in the search listings will pay long-term dividends, providing a flow of free, highly targeted visits for years to come.

> **Effort invested in making your website rank highly in the search listings will pay dividends.**

- **Pay-per-click** advertising is a perfect example of the way the internet has democratised marketing. Using a pay-per-click facility such as Google's Adwords, smaller businesses can trade on equal terms alongside big-brand rivals. What's more, the process can be instigated so quickly that new customers can sometimes be gained in under 15 minutes. Advertisers only pay when a visitor clicks through to their website. These visits tend to be of high quality because the visitor will have actively used keywords relevant to the destination website.
- **Online advertising.** Despite doubts about the effectiveness and popularity of banners and pop-ups, online advertising is coming close to achieving annual budget equality with traditional TV advertising. The techniques employed are constantly evolving as the internet itself becomes an increasingly more sophisticated medium and users become harder to impress. Online advertising is of natural interest to marketers due to its finely tuned targeting capability, real-time response possibilities, global reach and its ability to accurately measure the rate of response.

> **Online advertising is of natural interest to marketers due to its ability to target accurately and measure response.**

Summary

The internet is relatively new; however, the evergreen marketing rules that define a planned approach are still applicable. Have a strategy, understand your targets, continuously monitor progress and remain legal. Email offers the most viable direct marketing tool of the modern age. A web presence is a wise inclusion in the modern marketing arsenal. An online brochure is 'entry level' after which follow e-commerce and other interactivity. Social media is the new liberator for users and has healthy features for marketers. Blogs and Wikis can be very influential but should be approached with netiquette. Podcasts and video streaming give an interesting insight into where it's possibly all heading.

Also read sections: 3; 4; 27; 34; 44

34 Internet marketing

‘Barely 20 years old, this fabulous upstart has changed the way we live and buy – the shopportunity has only just begun.’

Those who think that the internet is hip should 'get with the program!' Not only is it old news – it's too old. At CERN, where Sir Tim Berners-Lee created the web in 1989, scientists are developing the Grid, which will revolutionise internet technology. Out will go old phone-style cables and routers, in will come streamlining fibre optics. Watch this space! Another opportunity marketers are already exploring is the social space called Second Life where alter egos can meet and interact virtually. Just how all this will affect use of the internet, as we know it, is not yet clear. Online real-world retail sales are predicted to reach £60 billion by 2010 so it does look like a case of onwards and upwards for web 2.0 and e-marketing.

- **Your website** is the essential starting point for serious online marketing ambitions. It must be reliably hosted to provide continuity and performance. It should be built for purpose, in line with your online marketing strategy. It should avoid potential stumbling blocks such as irritating pop-ups, frame construction and excessive animation. It should be search engine friendly and include a site map. It should also land confirmed shoppers on a buying page. Your website should be well designed, to compete favourably with others and to fit the expectations of your target market.

- **The target market** is becoming more important for web marketers who are finding that segmentation is just as helpful online as elsewhere. For example, if you are aiming to sell cars or dental services it is realistic to assume that buyers are unlikely to travel more than 40 miles, so your target audience must be segmented by location as well as by personal interest. If your cars are sporty or luxury models, or if your dentistry is cosmetic rather than medical, those factors should become part of your targeting criteria too.

  Segmentation is just as helpful online as elsewhere.

- **Research matters.** Careful study of your database will help you identify common features or personal preferences that can also define your target market and address it relevantly. For example, if your target audience is predominantly female and of a particular age group, the design style of your website should match their preferences and expectations. First impressions and familiar visual 'language' will help visitors feel at home. Wise web marketers will visit competitor sites to learn lessons and make comparisons.

- **The need to promote.** 'Build it and they will come' no longer works. The internet is a hugely competitive environment and winning the attention of paying customers requires effort. Select your website's key words and phrases carefully, use a domain name (www.address) that is descriptive and memorable. Promote your internet location in the same way you would promote an offline facility using PR and proactive techniques including email footers, business cards, letterheads, packaging and print-media advertising. Check with specialist publications for details of the latest techniques.

'Build it and they will come' no longer works.

- **News and newsletters.** Updated product news, special offers and new industry developments make perfect material to post on your website where all fresh material gets the thumbs-up from search engine crawlers. You can also send the same material out to customers in the form of emailed bulletins and newsletters – include a voucher or special offer to increase responses. E-bulletins provide a perfect opportunity to strengthen customer relationships and to keep your name, your offering and your personality alive in their minds.

- There are two key methods for **promoting yourself online**. The first is generally known as pay-per-click (PPC), in which advertisers pay for sponsored links from a search engine direct to their website. The advantage of PPC advertising is that advertisers only pay when a visitor actually clicks through to their site. Because the visitor would have found the advertiser by entering specific search criteria, clicked through traffic can be assumed to be relevant. As examples, Google AdWords, Yahoo! Search Marketing and Microsoft adCenter each offer comparable **pay-per-click** services.

There are two key methods for promoting yourself online.

- The second key promotional method is **Search Engine Optimisation** (SEO), which aims to achieve the best advertising position in the 'natural' (unsponsored) search engine listings. Successful SEO can be a complicated goal to reach. Google apparently uses over 200 markers to assess quality and status. Those markers include having carefully considered, high quality, keyword rich wording on your site and high quality, third party links with other relevant sites. Ultimately, the search engines decide ranking but having a SEO programme in place will help you.

- **Affiliate marketing** refers to the practice of rewarded referrals, in which company A will promote company B who will pay a commission (usually) if a sale results. Although they were not the first merchant to operate an affiliate programme, Amazon.com is one of the most frequently quoted examples. Amazon's affiliates promote books (for example) on their own websites. Interested customers are then linked with Amazon.com. If the customer buys the item from Amazon, the affiliate receives a commission.
- **Link strategies** are important. A link from another highly ranked website with similar subject matter will help your rankings. Always observe **Netiquette** – the unwritten rules of online promotion. Using underhand techniques or blasting your message without any thought to targeting could damage your brand in an environment where opinions can spread fast.

> **Using underhand techniques or blasting your message could damage your brand.**

- **Legalities** relating to e-commerce are important. Expert e-commerce lawyer Struan Robertson advises that all e-marketers should be aware of their legal obligations. Free information about the various UK laws that affect e-commerce can be found at *www.out-law.com.*

Summary

All predictions suggest that the culture of e-commerce will continue to grow. Build your website around a realistic online marketing strategy – and build that around your intended customers. Find out who, what and where they are by using research and current experience. Identify specific target segments. Actively promote your website, on and offline. Maintain customer contact with email and newsletters. Keep your website content fresh and updated. Investigate sponsored link strategies and search engine optimisation techniques. Also consider Affiliate schemes and Link strategies. Get into specialist blogs to soak up tips and remember to check your legal obligations.

Also read sections: 3; 6; 8; 12; 23; 33

35 In-house marketing

If your organisation is heavily into direct marketing you could be producing your own mailers – and impressing the accounts department too.

The term In-house Marketing (IHM) refers to the increasingly popular practice of producing marketing materials, most commonly leaflets and single-sheet flyers, within the office environment and without involving traditional or outsourced graphics or print suppliers. Thanks to continuing advances in digital technology, good quality colour printing is now achievable within the office environment. As the technology gets smarter the large, complex machinery that previously characterised commercial print supply has given way to neat, easily operated systems no bigger than the average photocopier. Work that used to take weeks can now be achieved in days using sophisticated electronic equipment. Importantly, the organisation has full control of the entire operation – including the turnaround time. This means that Monday's sales meeting idea can now become Tuesday's personalised mailshot.

> **The potential for IHM to produce cost savings is clear.**

- **IHM technology** comprises of a hybrid photocopier-cum-digital printer that uses sealed ink cartridges, so there are no messy cans of wet ink to worry about. The controlling software has been developed with office staff in mind, eliminating the necessity of high level skills training (allegedly). The upside is definitely about convenience and control. The inevitable downside is the balance between initial set-up cost and long-term savings. It is likely that those with a hefty and consistent requirement will make best gains. That said, though the potential for IHM to produce cost savings is clear, its ability to produce effective and strategic marketing materials is not so easily calculated.
- The main cost element with traditional printing is in the time it takes to initially set up the machine. Subsequently, the larger the printed quantity, the more economical the run becomes. IHM scores **best on shorter runs** where considerable cost savings can be made. Quantities of 1,000 or 1,500 can apparently be produced for around half the cost of traditional print, though the advantage diminishes as quantities increase due to the relatively high cost of IHM consumables.
- Time is another tempting advantage. Most traditional print shops will want at least a few days, if not a week, to turn a job around. IHM

systems will enable you to set up and implement most requirements in a few hours. Meaning that you are **in greater control** of your own project and that you can produce topical printed material very rapidly – for example, quick-fire promotional offers or bang up-to-date newsletters.

> Effectiveness rises by 500 per cent when the target's personal name or needs are highlighted.

- **Personalisation** of direct mail campaigns can be extremely effective. One recent estimate suggests that effectiveness rises by 500 per cent when the target's personal name, situation or needs are highlighted in the sales pitch – 'Dear Mr Smith, we can help you and Mrs Smith find your dream home in Kathmandu'. Another advantage of IHM is that you need not entrust your valuable customer database to an external mailing house.
- So, why would you want to go to all the trouble of generating mountains of paper sales material anyway? The simple answer is because it works. Despite all the benefits of the internet, good old-fashioned, tactile, direct mail still cuts the mustard. The paperless society didn't ever happen – in fact some estimates suggest that sales of A4 paper have increased by around 40 per cent since we all become computer focused. If paper is still persuasive, lower cost persuasion makes sense.
- How far you should go with DIY however is perhaps an issue. Whilst it might be tempting to do everything yourself it is nevertheless worth bearing in mind that, if you are not a professional **graphic designer**, whatever you produce could be doing more harm than good. One solution could be to get a professional designer to help you set up a template that you can adjust, update and reuse repeatedly. Many of the IHM hardware suppliers are offering ready-to-roll templates as part of their package.
- You may also benefit from some support from a professional **copywriter**. Alternatively, rather than hire professional specialist support, you could upskill those who will spearhead your IHM efforts. There are some very user-friendly graphics software packages available that, with practice, can enable non-professionals to achieve respectable results. Shop around until you find the best deal.
- The best way to tell how well your in-house efforts compare with professional written and designed materials is, firstly, by reviewing

their effectiveness – if they are generating good business for you there is no need to worry – and secondly, by comparison. Lay your stuff alongside your competitors' and see for yourself which works best. Be honest and realistic. It's better to be content with saving money on the print aspects alone rather than trying to cut every other corner too.

Lay your stuff alongside your competitors' and see which works best.

- Experiment with the paper stock you intend to use. Though you want in-house control and savings you presumably won't want to look home-made or cheap. Paper choice can make a world of difference to first impressions. The right combination of quality reproduction and paper can give you a result that is often hard to distinguish from traditional methods of printing. Remember that colour is much more effective than black and white and adding unique personalisation will make your mailing more relevant to the target – and consequently more effective. Try dividing your database – target one half with letterbox mail and the other half with email – to test which works best.

Target one half with letterbox mail and the other half with email.

Summary

There is little doubt that increased control and lower costs can both be achieved by adopting in-house marketing technology. However, care must be taken not to throw the baby out with the bathwater. Marketing communication is best defined not by how cheap it is but by how effective it is. With this in mind it might be prudent not to remove persuasive copywriting and skilled design from the equation just to please the accounts department. Weighing up the cost against the results will help you decide if IHM is the right tool for you. Anything that helps your marketing budget go further must be worth consideration.

Also read sections: 10; 20; 22; 24; 26; 30

36 Telemarketing

Don't hang up! In the hands of smart operators the telephone can help you turn cold contacts into hot prospects.

In a recent marketing campaign conducted by a friend, a well-written letter, including a free gift, was sent to prospects asking them to identify key business issues. Though they all kept the freebie very few of the prospects responded. Fortunately, the campaign planner had considered this possibility and had a team of telemarketing professionals standing by. In their first day of making follow-up calls to the same prospects the phone rangers tripled the success rate achieved over two weeks by the mailing. Proof, were it needed, that the telephone can be a significant marketing weapon, especially when wielded by experts. Whether the calls are made inbound to free-phone numbers or outbound to prospects, telemarketing offers an opportunity for direct contact, which can often be invaluable.

- Telemarketing provides an ideal means for reaching prospects quickly and easily. It is especially helpful where personal visits would be impractical and, unlike other marketing tools such as mailers or brochures, it offers the benefit of real time, two-way interaction. Telemarketing can be tightly targeted, organised and deployed rapidly, is instantly evaluated and relatively cost efficient. However, despite all these positive attributes, the telemarketing industry suffers from the potential for misuse.

- Professional telemarketer Karon Clark advises that the telephone is a great tool for qualifying prospects and for making sales to cold contacts. The trick is to form **realistic objectives** and to accept that the process may require more than one call, each building a bridge to the next. But you must be clear about your aims from the outset – do you want information, appointments or orders?

The trick is to form realistic objectives.

- There are two ways to approach telemarketing. The first is to ask a poorly paid, poorly informed, poorly trained, fast-talking chancer to make as many hit or miss phone calls to just about anybody, anywhere, in the vague hope that sooner or later somebody will say yes. It is this method that gets the other method a bad name. Alternatively, the professional approach begins with **research and**

preparation. Who do you want to talk with? What will interest them? What might switch them off? What questions might they ask you? How will you respond?

- The call can be won or lost in the **first 20 seconds**. During this time the caller will inspire just one of two emotions in the recipient: interest or resistance. Adequate preparation and a good sales pitch are essential: (1) **Be clear about your objective**; (2) **Know as much as possible** about the person you are calling and their relationship with your offering; (3) **Be prepared to be intercepted** by a screener; (4) **Plan your opening words** carefully, build in relevance to the recipient and clear benefits; (5) **Speak clearly**, confidently and at a moderate pace – avoid blurting and fake familiarity.

The caller will inspire just one of two emotions in the recipient.

- The very nature of telemarketing means that rejection is an ever-present possibility. Don't take it personally – you either have the wrong prospect or there's room for improvement with your opening line. The next call could be entirely different.

- A common hurdle for telemarketers is the **gatekeeper**. Their job is to screen their boss from interruptions. It is better to try and enlist their help rather than attempt to push past them. Tell them why your offering will benefit their boss and ask their advice on how and when you should make your approach. Don't say 'we make widgets, put me through', do say 'I have some new widgets that have helped others in your position to reduce cost/increase profits. I'm keen to ask Mr Boss a few questions to see if our widgets could work for you too. It might be an interesting opportunity for you'.

- The key to successful cold calling is credibility. You are unlikely to achieve it with a garbled machine gun pitch that sounds like it has been repeated a thousand times. **Each call must sound completely personal.** Listen to the phone calls you receive and note the voice styles that are calm, trustworthy, believable and non-threatening. Model your approach on their example. Also consider the pushy sales calls you have experienced, note the common, tired clichés and avoid them. Record yourself and continuously polish your telephone credibility.

- Telemarketing requires a contacts list. You can create your own or buy a ready-made database from a list broker (see Yellow Pages under direct mail or the Direct Marketing Association *www.dma.org.uk*). Your list should accurately match the prospect types you are interested in and it should be up-to-date. If you appoint a professional telemarketer, any list purchased should be obtained (and therefore owned) by you, not them. Check your obligations under the Data Protection Act.

- If you are uncertain about whether to hire a professional telemarketer try a test run. Remember, it's all about the quality of the results not the quantity of calls. If you hire professionals make sure your arrangement reflects this point. Telemarketing is a specialism requiring **experience, training and skill**. There's a lot to be said for letting the professionals get on with what they do best while you do likewise.

> There's a lot to be said for letting the professionals get on with what they do best.

- **There are regulations** controlling telemarketing activities. In the UK individuals can opt out of receiving unsolicited telephone calls by registering with the Telephone Preference Service (TPS). Businesses can do the same via the Corporate Telephone Preference Service (CTPS). Professional telemarketers are required to screen their databases for opt-out registrations. Ofcom will act against persistent misusers *www.ofcom.org.uk*. If you intend to DIY, check your legal situation first.

> If you intend to DIY, check your legal situation first.

Summary

Telemarketing can include inbound or outbound call handling. Outbound calls are usually aimed at producing leads, appointments or sales. The process may require more than one call. Begin with clear objectives and an understanding of what will win the interest of your target. The single word that separates a nuisance call from a beneficial outcome is credibility. Inbound or outbound, the opening sentences are the most important – don't rush, speak calmly and professionally. Rejection is a fact but it should not be taken personally. Learn how to win over gatekeepers. Buy or grow your own contacts list. Be aware of your responsibilities with data protection and TPS registrations.

Also read sections: 6; 8; 13; 14; 41

37 Sales promotion

'Incentivising and exciting additional sales can work in every market and in any medium – read now, while stocks last.'

A while back, an account manager in a London sales promotion agency created a special offer to enhance sales of a snacks brand. The deal was simple – buy a qualifying number of snacks and claim a free tracksuit. The programme was launched and sales rose. Soon the last tracksuit left the warehouse, marking the end of another successful project, except it wasn't the end. Having been told that his tracksuit application was void due to depleted stock, one customer correctly pointed out that 'while stocks last' was not mentioned in the promotional literature. The hapless account manager continued to personally provide tracksuits for weeks before he was finally fired. There are two lessons here. Firstly, that sales promotion can be very effective and secondly, that both sides should check the small print.

To stimulate sales or interest for a pre-planned, limited period.

- **Sales promotion** is one of the five important components of the promotional mix – the others being advertising, personal selling, direct marketing and public relations. Its role is to stimulate sales or interest for a preplanned, limited period. Sales promotion is commonly used in saturated or highly competitive market situations. It can be applied to encourage customer purchases (consumer promotion) and to excite trade or retail co-operation (trade promotion). Promotional techniques can also be employed internally (staff promotion) to incentivise higher productivity or to reward good performance.

- The underlying **purposes of sales promotion** activity can vary. Common aims include: creating awareness or encouraging trial of a new or improved product; clearing stocks of an old product; providing a periodic injection of fresh cash; increasing brand dominance or loyalty; smoothing out the effects of seasonal demand; unbalancing the competition; and creating news or simply recruiting new customers.

- Familiar **sales promotion techniques** can be seen in most supermarkets, in both on- and offline stores and in much of the regular press. There are five common categories: (1) Cash incentives – discounts, savings and vouchers; (2) Bonus schemes – loyalty awards, extra goods or services, trade-up deals; (3) Promotional gifts – free samples, free gift with purchase, business gifts; (4) Prize promotions – competitions, prize draws, scratch cards; (5) Collector schemes – collect tokens, collect bonus points, collect incremental parts.

Cash incentives, bonus schemes, promotional gifts, prize promotions, collector schemes.

- All customer offers and advantages provided during sales promotion activity are **special offers** in the sense that they incentivise extraordinary sales activity to occur in short-term bursts, which run for a limited period. Promoters should be able to demonstrate that special offers are genuinely out of the ordinary and time bound. For example, winter or summer sales will excite and generate special interest but an all-year-round sale would not be credible.

- There is no sales or customer communication channel where sales promotion techniques cannot be applied. Online promotions observe similar principles to those encountered in the high street, though the delivery mechanic will differ of course. Given that the whole point of sales promotion is, by and large, to boost sales, it is perhaps unsurprising that considerable promotional activity occurs at or near the point-of-sale itself or alternatively at the point-of-decision, where the buying outcome can be most effectively influenced.

The whole point of sales promotion is to boost sales.

- **Example 1**: A blinds and awnings manufacturer is annually swamped by high demand in spring, when customers traditionally begin focusing on patio activity and conservatories. However, the company needs to retain its staff and survive with little income throughout the winter months. They adopt sales promotion techniques to stimulate off-season orders, offering discounted prices, extended payment terms and value added extras such as a free design and measuring service.

- **Example 2**: To encourage its members to recommend that their friends and relatives become members, the AA offers complimentary Marks & Spencer vouchers as a reward. The existing members are mailed four tokens to distribute to their personal contacts. Each token carries an identifying code which ensures that the referring member is rewarded whenever a token is submitted by a membership applicant. The applicants also receive the same reward, thus ensuring that the token is used. The physical evidence – the number of redeemed tokens – allows the success of the scheme to be monitored accurately.

- **Example 3**: British Airways is currently offering a series of downloadable podcasts on the topic of sleep – an important issue for air travellers. The podcasts offer is not linked specifically to a sale but can nevertheless be seen as a sales promotion because it connects customers and potential customers with the BA website, thus building awareness and enhancing BA's customer database.

- Sales promotion techniques can be used to encourage buyers of both **products and services**. Before nominating the activity decide what outcomes you are aiming for. Where possible, link the incentives you offer with your own brand activity rather than an unrelated third party. For example, Homebase keep customers focused on their core offering by providing genuine periodic discounts for loyalty-card holders, rather than added-value giveaways of tins of salmon or suntan lotion.

- In the UK, **sales promotion is regulated by law**. Particular care should be taken when using the word 'free' and with the distinction between a competition (involving skill and judgement) and gambling. Marketer Jas Bains emphasises the requirement to display promotional terms and conditions where appropriate. These must be clear and concise so that there is no confusion about what is on offer, for how long and under what circumstances. The Institute of Sales Promotion *www.isp.org.uk* offers guidance and best practice notes. Articles and contacts can be found in Sales Promotion Magazine *www.salespromo.co.uk.*

Particular care should be taken when using the word 'free'.

Summary

Sales promotion techniques boost sales or attract attention for limited periods. Similar methods can be used for consumer, trade and staff promotions. Sales promotion techniques vary and can adapt to a wide range of purposes. Wise promoters identify the required outcome before the delivery technique. The principles of common methods can be observed in most supermarkets. Much promotional activity is focused at the point-of-sale or the point-of-decision. Sales promotion applies in all marketing channels and can work for both product and services markets. Promotional activity is regulated by law – take particular care with competitions. It is recommended that you seek specialist legal advice prior to organising DIY campaigns.

Also read sections: 12; 13; 21; 28; 42

38 Word-of-mouth marketing

‘If creating new customers is part of your marketing ambition, then encouraging those who value you to become ambassadors makes perfect sense.’

In the not too distant past having one customer recommend you to another was seen either as a pleasant surprise or a random bonus – the kind of unexpected windfall that restores your faith in human nature. But times have changed. We now see highly specialised agencies forming around the concept of word-of-mouth – WOM – marketing. Business schools too have both seen and seized the opportunity. Dr Barry Ardley of Lincoln University advises that you should be aware that your ‘referral market’ can include more than customers. Other firms and professionals you deal with can help to enhance the reputation of your business through word-of-mouth marketing. Clearly the case for WOM has substance. What's more, it represents one of the lowest cost promotional options of all.

Why pay to advertise when others could do it for you?

- According to research, 75 per cent of us trust personal recommendations more than we trust advertising. Consequently, any product or service news that arrives by word-of-mouth via an acquaintance or a peer is more likely to be treated favourably and acted upon. It is perhaps unsurprising then, that the marketing industry has honed the potential for harnessing and managing the process of infectious personal endorsements. Why pay to advertise when, with a prompt, others could do it for you?

- The activity has attracted an array of descriptions including WOM, influencer marketing, positive buzz, ambassador programmes, viral spread and more. Those who are primed or encouraged to spread the word are variously known as advocates, envoys, activators, adopters, influencers and sneezers.

Word-of-mouth has two very different threads, which should be understood.

- Word-of-mouth philosophy has engendered two very different threads, which should be separately understood. The first is the **referral system**. This aims to encourage known customers, colleagues or suppliers to give favourable recommendations about your products or services to their own contacts. Thus generating more opportunities for you.

- The second thread is **influencer marketing**, which sets out to identify selected individuals and prime them to influence potential buyer groups on your behalf. Both the referral system and influencer marketing can, and should, be systematically approached and evaluated. However, influencer marketing can be highly structured and is the variant most likely to require specialist support.

- An example of the **referral system**: a firm of mortgage brokers will seek new business opportunities from recommendations given by a neighbouring firm of accountants. The accountants identify potential mortgage seekers from their own client list and suggest to those clients that they should make contact with the broker. Alternatively, the accountant will pass the clients' details to the broker who will contact them directly. Either way, the broker will probably offer the accountant some kind of reward incentive for their efforts – and to encourage future efforts. The incentive might be a tangible reward or reciprocal referrals.

- The **referral system** should not be left to chance. It can be turned into an ongoing process using the following steps: (1) Set a target that is appropriate for your circumstances. For example, you could aim for three referrals per week or per month; (2) Identify satisfied customers who are likely to refer you; (3) Ask actively and specifically for the referral – 'I'm pleased that you are happy with our work, who else do you know who would be interested to learn about us?' If appropriate you could ask for a specific number of names, five perhaps; (4) Confirm the approach – ask 'Will you contact them yourself (if so, when) or would you prefer that I contact them and mention your name (if so, can I have their details)?' The second approach option might give you more control over the situation; (5) Measure the outcome against your targets.

- An example of **influencer marketing**: preparing for the launch of a new feminine product, a pharmaceutical company identified 50 influencers who were representative of the target audience and willing to attend a pre-launch event – a carefully managed party with plenty of indulgent luxuries. The product and its beneficial attributes were the real focus of the event, the aim being to create a 'buzz' about it and a bond among the influencers. Free samples were liberally distributed for the influencers to share with friends and contacts. A second event

> **The company ensured that hundreds of customers were familiar with their product.**

was arranged and the influencers were asked to attend and, this time, bring a friend. Lifestyle and female media professionals were also invited, along with a celebrity host to add sparkle. The second event repeated the party atmosphere and provided a very positive experience, which inevitably became associated through the influencers to the product itself. By repeating this process in several locations the pharmaceutical company ensured that hundreds of customers were primed and favourably familiar with their product by the launch date.

Don't assume that influencers will talk about you – prompt them.

- The **influencer marketing** process works this way: (1) Identify the influencers – those with the potential to influence the opinions of likely buyers; (2) Set targets for the number of buyers you want and the number of influencers the task will require; (3) Market to the influencers – give them a reason to be interested in you and something to say about you; (4) Market through the influencers – give them the tools to carry your message; (5) Measure the outcome against targets. At Step 3 **be sure to ask** influencers to talk about you, don't assume they will automatically do so.
- You should not attempt to control what referrers or influencers say about you. Their message on your behalf will carry more weight if it is expressed in their own way. Find our more at *www.womuk.org*.

Summary

Word-of-mouth marketing can include the referral system and influencer marketing. Both rely on personal endorsement or empathy, which is more effective than overt advertising. The referral system aims to obtain direct person-to-person recommendations from known customers or contacts. Influencer marketing aims to reach pre-qualified target groups by using the influencer as a conduit. In both cases the objective includes getting your product or service discussed and endorsed by others in a favourable context. Referrers must be thanked – possibly rewarded. Positive influence will only occur if the influencer is personally won over by your offering. Unlike referrers, influencers are not necessarily customers or known contacts.

Also read sections: 9; 11; 19; 21; 31; 40

39 Mobile marketing

The day of the digital nomad has arrived. With no wires tying them down customers (and marketers) can function on the move.

Years back, a friend, having tired of shovelling corporate guano, set off for rural France with his partner. Things worked out, but then they reached another bold conclusion – ditch the house! Home is now a camper and the address is anywhere in Europe. Soon they will be at a music festival in Corsica, just the four of them – him, her, the laptop and the mobile phone. Don't think I'm talking about some aimless drifter. The gentleman I refer to is the genius behind a web business that receives a million monthly visits. Management and admin are conducted on the move using the mobile as the vital connection. Alongside the internet, the development of the mobile phone has changed habits and provides an exciting opportunity for marketers.

Three-quarters of the human race will own a mobile by the end of 2012.

- Trade body The Mobile Data Association informs us that the potential for mobile marketing began in 1995 when SMS (short message service or 'text') was launched commercially. By 2007, SMS volumes had grown by 40 per cent per year – 6 billion text messages were sent in December alone. The number of picture messages – 448,962,359 – sent in 2007 equalled 19 million rolls of traditional camera film! According to market research from Portico Research, three-quarters of the human race will own a mobile handset by the end of 2012.

- Beyond enabling phone calls most modern mobile phones can capture, send and receive picture images and video clips. Files can be routed through the mobile networks or via the internet. Thanks to fast data transfer provided by 2.5 G (GPRS) and 3G (third generation) wireless technology, the mobile phone is now also an internet access tool. Other wireless hand-held devices such as the BlackBerry and PDAs also have this capability. Laptop users can connect to the worldwide web via their mobile or wi-fi connection. Bluetooth technology is available on most modern devices and allows for transfer of data wirelessly, free of charge, without connection to a network.

- **SMS (short message service)**. Since the first campaign, run by Labatt in 2002, SMS or text messaging has become an established marketing tool, being used for competitions, promotions, television voting and so forth. Specific examples include: weekly bank mini-statements; rail service updates; and health appointment reminders. Its strengths are in simplicity, immediacy, low costs and potentially broad reach. A valuable feature for marketers is that text messaging is commonly used in communication between friends, therefore it is not perceived as obtrusive – recipients will respond and engage more freely.

- **MMS (multimedia message service)**. Also known as picture messaging, this feature of mobile phones enables users to capture and send picture and video messages together with text and audio. Most new handsets are enabled to receive and send pictures or multimedia messages. The ability to instantly self-record, then share life experiences has proved popular, especially with youth markets.

- **Personal mobile gaming** is by no means a novel matter for younger mobile users who take simple casual games in their stride. Technology is increasing the potential for interactive 3D games, multi-player games and social network games. Versions of all these, tailored to older or more specialised audiences are likely. Marketers can deliver promotional messages within the game or by sponsoring it overtly.

- **LBS (location-based services).** Using a variety of methods mobile network operators can identify the location of the handset. For marketers this provides an opportunity to send location-specific information to the mobile user. Examples include: travel guides; hotel information; translation services; currency converters; flight offers; car hire info; and even tourist attraction offers or shopping vouchers.

- **CRM (customer relationship management)** is a marketing technique not confined to mobile telephones. However, the immediacy and person-to-person capabilities of the mobile channel make it a strong contender for CRM programs. I was once delighted to receive a CRM text message advising that 'Your AA patrol will reach you in ten minutes'. Other uses include: weather updates; personal greetings; confirmation of orders; notification of special offer prices; thought for the day; 'thank you for your business'; satisfaction surveys; and voting.

The capabilities of the mobile channel make it a strong contender for CRM programs.

- **MVM (mobile viral marketing)** invites a recipient to transmit a message or file onwards to members of their peer group or social network. Those recipients are, in turn, expected to continue the spread of the 'virus'. Depending on the nature of, or the quality of, the message recipients will either decide naturally to pass it on or else they may have to be prompted. Popular themes for viral seeding are music, ringtones, sponsored jingles, humour, graphics and carefully targeted promotional offers – for example, event tickets or theme-store discounts.

- **Mobile internet.** According to The Mobile Data Association, 17 million people – almost one quarter of UK mobile users – accessed the internet via their mobile in December 2007. In the same month Vodafone customers rated their most popular top-five internet sites as: (1) Facebook; (2) Sky; (3) Google; (4) The BBC; and (5) MSN. There is still work to be done in addressing consumer concerns over access price and in developing more adaptable web-to-mobile interfaces but, notwithstanding these teething problems, the mobile phone surely has a big future.

> **17 million people accessed the internet via their mobile in December.**

- The Mobile Marketing Association (MMA) has established a recognised code of conduct for the mobile marketing industry. The code, together with information and advice can be found at *www.mmaglobal.com*. The Mobile Data Association reflects the common voice of the industry and can be found at *www.themda.org*.

> **The mobile telephone provides fantastic opportunities for direct, interactive contact with unique targets.**

Summary

The mobile telephone has come a long way. For marketers it provides the best possible opportunity for direct, interactive contact with unique targets. Mobile telephones provide marketers with several options: SMS – short message service – better known as 'text' messaging; MMS – multimedia service – in and outbound picture, word, audio and video messaging; Personal mobile gaming – simple, interactive or multi-player games; LBS – location-based services – real-time, geographically relevant information; CRM – customer relationship management – via (predominantly) SMS; MVM – mobile viral marketing – 'pass-it-on' messages into and through peer groups; Mobile internet – access to the web from the handset or the mobile laptop.

Also read sections: 3; 11; 28; 37; 44

CHAPTER SEVEN

Tools, tips and time-savers

In this chapter:

40. **Networking** – make sure that your networking IS working properly
41. **Vital statistics** – surveys and questionnaires – YES, NO, MAYBE and how
42. **Sales literature** – what it is, what's important, what's not and why not
43. **Press advertising** – what works best and what's best to avoid
44. **Working with techies** – Earth calling webmaster, come in please, over
45. **Working with creatives** – please don't cry, it's lovely, honestly!
46. **Hiring consultants** – the pros and cons of high quality professional support
47. **Hiring freelancers** – making music with one-man-bands
48. **Buying print** – the possibilities and pleasures of paper and ink
49. **Negotiating** – critical moves for buyers, sellers and survivors

40 Networking

Not everyone is a natural networker, but with a little effort and a personal strategy we can all reap rewards.

Management mastermind Peter Drucker observed that '*More business decisions occur over lunch and dinner than at any other time, yet no MBA courses are given on the subject*'. Drucker of course was way ahead of his time and some business schools now incorporate networking with their curriculum. His comment reminds us of two pertinent features from the phenomenon of **business networking.** Firstly, that being out of the office and exploring social exchange can encourage relationships and relaxed, productive thinking. Secondly, that for some, the ritual does not come easy and requires assistance, even education. The once 'not very British' trend for business networking has now become eminently acceptable and represents an enjoyable, low-cost marketing option with great potential for those who 'boldly go . . .'

One networker achieved sales worth £200,000 from just one network group.

- There can be few business people who have not experienced some form of networking. Google offers over 24,000 results, including options for breakfast, lunch and evening. Even those who find it difficult to leave their desks need not miss out because **online networks are also available**. Does it work? One networker quoted in *The Times* achieved sales worth £200,000 from just one network group. That said, expert Heather White, author of the book ***Networking for Business Success***, proposes that networking is not just about selling, it is also about developing confidence, gleaning intelligence and even simply making friends.

- **It's not what you know but who you know.** Success in business often depends on having the right contacts. Networking is the perfect mechanism because those who get involved are keen to meet new faces. They might be complete strangers but don't forget that a stranger is only a potentially valuable contact who you haven't yet met.

- A survey carried out by Essex Chambers of Commerce asked attendees of several networking groups **what they expected to gain**. Answers included: the opportunity to promote my business; insight into how other businesses work; to find out what's going on; useful and motivating business presentations; social contacts and possibly new friends. And crucially – new connections and more business.

> **The opportunity to find new friends, new connections and more business.**

- The same survey also asked attendees **what aspects of networking they liked least**: pushy people loading you up with leaflets; cliques who won't mix; early morning meetings; juggling plate, glass, bag and business cards; people who are blatantly only interested in me if I'm of use to them; the same old faces; the time and effort it takes; people who hound you; wasted events with no useful contacts; IT people who speak another language (there are lessons here).

- The research usefully identified **the most liked aspects of networking**: meeting people and sharing experiences; learning; great for those who work from home; a sounding-board for ideas; sense of community; meeting on a sociable level; it's about people, not just about a sales pitch; being able to give referrals. One notable respondent reflected, 'I liked the food, the tea and the biscuits'.

- **Fear can be an issue for some.** The survey revealed several examples of personal dread: I feel self-conscious and awkward; walking into a room full of strangers; starting a conversation with a stranger; not being able to break away. Networking isn't natural for everybody – but **fear can often be controlled** with a pre-event strategy. Don't leave it until you arrive.

- The way to reduce nerves and increase your effectiveness is to **develop a personal success strategy**. This will help reduce fear of the unknown and put you in control. Write down the things you want to achieve and then treat this as a brief to yourself. For example, you could brief yourself to meet at least three people or to not be worried about exiting a conversation if it is uncomfortable. Brief yourself to use an exit strategy – 'It's been nice chatting but please excuse me, there's somebody I want to catch before they leave'.

> **This will help reduce fear of the unknown and put you in control.**

- **Good networking habits** . . . Keep to a narrow range of clothing styles so that people recognise you each time. Take the time to introduce others, regardless of whether there's a gain for you. Travel light so as not to physically encumber yourself. Be pleasant and diplomatic – you never know who, knows who, knows who. Try to leave each conversation with an agreed action – I'll call you no later than . . .'. It makes sense to endear yourself to the event organisers too. Always introduce yourself and offer to help if they are pushed.

There is a fine line between spreading useful information and becoming a pest.

- **Bad habits to avoid** . . . Be meticulous over personal etiquette – you cannot possibly make a favourable impression with foul breath or body odour. Nor will you do yourself any favours if you pin people into a corner and berate them. Talking to people whilst simultaneously eating or drinking needs to be watched as does barging into somebody's personal space or private conversation. There is a fine line between spreading welcome and useful information and becoming a pest by pressing your literature onto people who might not be interested.
- **Networking tips include**: focus on relationships – opportunities and benefits will soon follow; talk to the keynote speaker before the event – they'll be busy afterwards; take the 5Bs – boldness, business cards, breath fresheners, biro and badge; if you're nervous – be early; try to help first-timers and wallflowers; don't brag or bad-mouth others; ask open questions; smile for at least two minutes on the way to the event – it helps your natural smile. Remember – **you don't always need an event to be a brilliant networker**. You can network any time, anywhere, using the phone or email.

Summary

It's not just who you know, but who they know too. Mature networkers make connections and onward referrals. They also focus on relationships rather than a brief opportunity to swap business cards. Good networkers are often natural 'people' people. If a room full of strangers intimidates you focus on one-to-one networking. Write your strategy for success and let it be your guide. Decide what you want to achieve in advance and don't leave until you achieve it. Perfect your elevator speech, be helpful to novices and don't feel obliged to stick with boors. Personal hygiene is important, along with the ability to offer a welcoming smile.

Also read sections: 2; 6; 7; 12; 13; 21; 38

41 Vital statistics

Can satisfaction surveys and questionnaires help you move forward? Answer: strongly disagree, disagree, agree, agree strongly – or other!

'*Figures won't lie, but liars will figure.*' Charles H. Grosvenor reminds us that if we want to know what's going on, relying on the view of just one or two people could be risky. We need to consult multiple opinions and we have learned to do it using evaluation forms, happy sheets, polls, surveys and questionnaires. Their purpose is to help organise the collection of data that can be turned into useful information. Specifically, surveys can be used to: check customer awareness (of a product or service for example); evaluate satisfaction (of a service or an event perhaps); capture opinions (about policy or change maybe); track trends and habits (to spot future strategies); measure competitive performance (how are you better, worse or different). The possibilities are endless.

There are four main survey methods and each has its own strengths.

- **There are four main survey methods**: telephone; postal; face-to-face; and internet. Each has its own strengths and weaknesses. The telephone enables very fast results, permits flexible questioning and can provide high response rates but it can also be costly. Postal surveys offer low cost and they can helpfully depersonalise the response, but they also tend to provide low response rates (unless incentivised) and offer no means to clarify answers. Face-to-face surveys enable easy target type confirmation and the opportunity to study body language. But they are time consuming and consequently expensive. Email and online surveys can be deployed very rapidly and carry the obvious advantage of enabling a potentially global reach. They are highly cost effective too but can also stumble with unreliable response rates.

- Questioning styles can vary. Direct questions are openly about the respondent while indirect questions ask the respondent about the behaviour or preferences of others. Open questions usually invite free-ranging answers while closed questions confine responses to, for example, yes, no or not sure. Multiple choice questioning techniques can be useful in obtaining data quickly, though they might not allow for subtle replies unless very carefully written. Scaled score questions give the respondent the opportunity to specify an answer on variable levels – for example, 'How satisfied are you on a scale of one (poor) to five (excellent)?'.

- Before constructing your survey define precisely what you need to know. Ask yourself what information will move you forwards. Once you know what you need to know, forming the questions and selecting the most appropriate questioning style will be much easier. Are you looking for measurable (quantitative) responses such as 22 per cent of participants prefer blue or 8 out of 10 say we are fairly priced. Or are you looking for more emotional (qualitative) replies along the lines of 'Blue reminds me of . . .' or 'Future topics that would interest me include . . .'.

- Unless you are gathering diverse opinions to gain a big picture, your data will be easier to evaluate if the questions are put consistently and with as little room for misinterpretation as possible. ALWAYS test surveys on an uninitiated sample group before deploying them. It is best to expose any flaws or ambiguities and correct them before the survey goes live. Denise Rossiter, who oversees data collection for the Chambers of Commerce, warns that care must be taken to avoid 'loading' questions in a way that might undermine the credibility of the response.

ALWAYS test surveys on an uninitiated sample group before deploying.

- In telephone and face-to-face situations qualify the suitability of the subject at the outset. For example, asking, 'Are you a car driver?' will confirm that your subject is appropriate for a survey on vehicle insurance. If the answer is no you can move on to another person. It can also be helpful to state at the start roughly how long the interview will take. This will help prevent losing a subject who has to rush off before completing it. Putting the easy or enjoyable questions at the beginning will help relax your subject and retain their interest.

- With non-assisted surveys it is vital that the questions are clear and easy to follow. Phyllis Laurence of Delgat Data Entry offers this advice: Be consistent with the layout of tick boxes and free text (handwritten replies), for example, keep tick boxes on the right and free text on the left. Tick-box responses provide unambiguous data that is quick and easy to capture and evaluate. Keep free text to a minimum because it can be costly to interpret, especially if the handwriting is hard to read.

Keep free text to a minimum because it can be costly to interpret.

- All data capture professionals urge that less is more. Fewer survey questions will usually guarantee more co-operative respondents and more completed forms. When seeking to capture name and address details make sure to leave adequate space for abnormally long surnames or long addresses. Always 'fence-off' a space for the postcode.
- Beware of gummed edges on paper data returns. If the data is too close to the gummed edge it will be at risk when the edges are separated. Gummed edge responses can take extra time (cost) to open and sometimes stick to each other. With online surveys remember to check the forms each day to ensure the fields are working and that there are no broken links.
- Remember, if you collect personal data from your survey contributors you should check your responsibilities under the Data Protection Act. You should also inform your contributors that their personal data will not be sold or gifted to a third party (assuming that this is so).

Check your responsibilities under the Data Protection Act.

Summary

Surveys provide data that can be turned into useful information – not to mention competitive advantage. Data can be obtained by personal interviews, either by telephone or face-to-face, or else in writing by post or via the internet. Do be clear about what information will move you forward before you select the method or create the survey intended to collect it. Also remember to test your survey before deploying it. Don't make your survey so long that it puts people off and don't forget to pre-qualify your contributor's relevance to the survey before going too far. Remember your obligations under the Data Protection Act.

Also read sections: 2; 3; 4; 5; 6; 13

42 Sales literature

‘The glossy gallery of paper paraphernalia that tells the world who you are, what you do and where you can be found.’

Any written works that explain or promote your organisation could be categorised as sales literature. The most commonplace examples include: brochures; product sheets; leaflets; flyers; handouts; catalogues; and newsletters. The term sales literature is usually applied to printed matter but there's no reason to fix on that idea, especially as most of the items listed above have 'e' equivalents. Though there is an obvious difference between paper and internet media, the same generic rules for good communication should apply – including that which states that one size seldom fits all. Whether you call it sales literature or marketing literature, the implication is almost the same. Ultimately, the purpose it fulfils is to reduce the distance between you and your potential customers and, in some cases, to enable actual purchases.

Visualise your customer, give them a name and bring them to life.

- Before you create another piece of sales literature consider this. What do you do with the junk mail that turns up at home or all the uninvited email that lands at your in-box? You probably bin more than you read, right? The one thing that will prompt you to stop and read stuff you never requested is **relevance**. If it grabs your attention by being relevant to your wants and needs then it has almost done its job. If you want effective sales literature follow **Rule 1 – Make it relevant to the recipient**. Expert Claire Lindsay recommends virtual profiling – visualise your customer, give them a name and bring them to life so that you can talk more directly to them.

- You can only be relevant if you pitch your offering at buyers' real needs – which means that you should know what those needs are before you start constructing your pitch. The beautifully engineered edges on your flagship widget might be important to you but they could be insignificant to a prospective buyer who might be more concerned about colour or price. **Accurate customer research is vital**.

- Sales literature acts as your silent ambassador, representing you or your organisation when you can't be present in person. Make sure the look and feel of your material is representative of the calibre of your offering. The purpose of sales literature is: to gain attention; to prompt a response; to prompt the response you want.

- Less is invariably more. Keep the front page as punchy as possible, avoid unnecessary detail. The job of the cover or front page is to attract, then hint at the benefits to come, not to explain the full story. Remember that the more you put in, the harder you will make it for the viewer to digest. Aim to keep the proposition – the expression of the offer – simple and to the point. **Single-minded propositions are more effective** than multi-tiered ones.

- What works on paper might not work online. Online readers require a shorter, more rapid experience than those handling paper, who are inclined to dwell a little longer, so long passages of text work better offline. Touch becomes more important too as paper quality, texture or thickness adds a different tactile dimension. Paper invokes tactile involvement with interesting folds, and even smells.

Paper can invoke tactile involvement with interesting folds, and even smells.

- Sales text must get to the point but always aim to talk '**with**' the reader rather than '**at**' them. Avoid using words that merely describe, instead use vigorous words that paint a picture or inspire a sensation. Rather than say 'This is a cake', try 'This delicious cake absolutely oozes sweet sensations'. Rather than say 'The FTSE fell sharply', say 'The FTSE plummeted'.

- Never assume that readers know what you know. Avoid technical jargon and elitism or anything else that might create a barrier to quick and easy understanding. Always get an uninvolved reader to give feedback on what you've produced – before you publish it. Remember that you are responsible for what you release into the public domain. You must not mislead or give offence.

- Successful sales literature is built on customer benefits, which can be expressed as text or bullet points or both. Testimonial statements from happy past-purchasers can add a reassuring touch. The 'call-to-action' – or the closing nudge that incites the reader to take action, pick up the phone or otherwise buy into the offering – is essential. All sales literature should spell out a clear pathway to purchase – don't just state your offering, lead buyers to it.

Don't just state your offering, lead buyers to it.

- Anything you can do to set a mood, incite an emotion or depict a benefit is good – especially if it helps reduce worded descriptions which take longer to digest and disseminate. Therefore, pictures are a boon but be aware that photography tends to be trusted more than illustration. Suggestive photography can inspire fun, trust, contentment, and other powerful emotional responses in a way that could perhaps challenge illustration. When in doubt, test both.
- Be aware that photography obtained from commercial photo libraries is usually priced according to the likely use. If you exceed the usage you have agreed to pay for you could find yourself in trouble. Remember that you cannot help yourself to images you might find hanging around in books or magazines or on the internet without putting yourself at risk of prosecution for copyright theft. When in doubt seek legal advice.
- When deciding what type of sales literature to produce; before selecting your best headline option; when considering colours, photography or illustrative styles; before beginning the design; before putting your logo at the top of the front page; before including a photo of yourself – apply Rule 1.

Before including a photo of yourself – apply Rule 1.

Summary

Consider these checkpoints: Why are you doing it – what do you want it to achieve? How can you be sure it will do so? Where will you put it and why? Have you tested it? Is it aligned with your organisational values? Will it meet the needs of your sales team? Will you need specialist professionals such as a writer, designer or photographer? What will it cost? Does it have visual impact alongside equivalent competitor pieces? Has the content been checked and double-checked for text errors? Are the phone and contact details current, correct and unlikely to change? Are dates or prices mentioned – could they change?

Also read sections: 10; 14; 20; 24; 26

43 Press advertising

You can't believe everything you read – except this round-up of what works best and what's best avoided.

As Canadian educator Laurence V. Peter (he of the Peter Principle) quipped – '*Early to bed, early to rise, work like hell and advertise!*' He had a point, after all the best widget in the world will stay on the shelf if nobody knows about it. Advertising, in one form or another, is still big business and has set the standard for reaching a wide audience without using motion picture media. Its attraction lies in the fact that it is relatively quick to organise and is accessible. There are two important features to take on board. Firstly, circulation figures of say 40,000 readers do not guarantee that you will sell 40,000 widgets. Secondly, that AIDA remains alive and valid (and is explained in this section).

- Broadly, **the options include** local press, national press, trade press and specialist press. Each has its own plus and minus points – national press reaches a wider audience than local press but is more expensive for advertisers. Magazines and periodicals will have less demanding deadlines but will take longer to reach customers. Small Ads work better in trade or specialist magazines because they are read more thoroughly. Glossy and lifestyle magazines will require quality design or photography.

- **Targeting and timing** are important. Consider these questions: Who are your best customers? Why do they come to you? What message will attract more like them? Where should that message be placed? Be ready with your Ad if what you sell is seasonal, for example, beachwear for holidays. Capitalise on anything that promotes interest in your type of business, such as Mother's Day perhaps. Learn what the media is focused on and be prepared to advertise alongside relevant features.

Who are your customers? What message will attract them? Where should that message be placed?

- **Never blow your budget** on one huge Ad. Frequency is safer, here's why. You can divide your audience into three groups: those who don't notice the Ad; those who aren't interested in it; and those who might be. Your Ad is likely to

Divide your audience into three groups: those who don't; those who aren't; and those who might.

appeal only to one-third of the readership – some experts suggest a ratio of one in five! Smaller, more frequent Ads will improve your chances. The same principle applies to media choice. Unless you're certain that your audience will be reading just one publication it is wise to put your message into several.

- AIDA, also known as the Hierarchy of Effects, describes the process of a sale. It is therefore a good template for how an Ad should work. A=Attention – if you don't capture that you fail. I=Interest – convert attention into deeper personal engagement with benefits or relevance. D=Demand – move the reader from interest to a 'must have' mindset. A=Action – don't leave readers poised but prompt a final step of commitment.

- **Successful Ads** are 'quick' to evaluate so minimise content. Include only elements that earn their keep. A single background colour will help you dominate the space you have paid for. If you must use horizontal blocks of colour put a holding keyline around the whole Ad to keep it contained. Be careful of white backgrounds – they can be affected by 'show-through' from overleaf.

- Before you approve the design **view it in context** – on a page amongst other Ads and at the final actual size rather than isolated and enlarged on a screen. Never let the publication prepare your Ad without seeing a proof before it's printed. If in doubt, look at example Ads that work well and aim for a similar recipe. Avoid overload – the more you put in, the less inviting your Ad will be.

- Invariably, the most important element of any Ad is **the headline**. It should immediately say to the reader 'HEY YOU – STOP!' It must be relevant to them – not about you. Don't start with your logo (who cares?) or with something like *'Bloggs and Co., excellence in management training since 1812'*. Instead, couch the offering in a way that is about the reader – *'You can earn more, work less and enjoy your job'*. The offering – management training – is the same, but the pitch is focused on the customer. Don't put a full stop at the end of a headline; it will prompt readers to break off.

- The publication's ratecard will explain sizes, costs, deadlines and technical requirements. If you want your Ad in a particular part of the publication (specified position) it will cost more than an Ad that goes wherever there's a gap (run-of-paper). Right-hand pages are supposedly more effective than left-hand and some experts suggest above the fold is better still. Check for discounts. If you are planning multiple insertions in varied publications consider involving a Media Buyer who will leverage discounts and handle logistics. If you submit your own Ads never assume that the artwork arrived or that it will print as you intended.

- Display Ad space (quarter, half and full page) starts at around ten times the cost of classified space (single column width by variable depth). You can make really crafty use of classified space using a spot colour. Publications often have unsold Ad spaces (remnant space) that they sell off cheap to anyone with an Ad ready to go – make sure they call you. If your Ad has a coupon ask for space at the edge of a page. Find a way of identifying responses and measuring how effective your Ads are.

Publications often have unsold Ad space that they sell-off cheap.

Even a brilliant Ad won't work in the wrong place.

Summary

A brilliant Ad won't work in the wrong place – focus on targeting the right people via the right media. Consider frequency and timing carefully. Don't overlook Media Buyers. Always supply artwork files with fonts and pictures embedded. Check that you have appropriate reproduction rights for images. Check the Advertising Standards Authority guidelines for conduct and content. Don't leave everything to the last minute. Double-check phone numbers, web addresses and other contact details. The Press Advertising environment is a busy, noisy, bustling place where dull Ads are easily overlooked – test your Ad (in context) for impact and performance.

Also read sections: 4; 8; 10; 24; 26; 29

44 Working with techies

> *Earth calling webmaster . . . come in webmaster. Some technical people might come across as alien but don't worry, they come in peace.*

The guys and gals who help the rest of us put the 'e' in e-marketing, the pro in programming and the wonder into websites are the stars of today's show, often treading a difficult path in creating solutions that appear simple, using technology that is anything but. Most of them are perfectly normal and don't shrivel up at sunrise or run away from garlic. Their technical skills have opened new frontiers and quite literally brought new dimensions to marketing. That said, the language barrier can sometimes be an issue, as can the gulf between too much technical understanding and too little. These frustrations can affect those on both sides of the digital divide, but then, nobody ever said that the revolution would be easy.

- **Modern marketing** relies on computers and the internet for much of its reach and operational ability. Digital dominance is here to stay and along with it has come a comparatively new evolutionary – the techie. Their roles include building the technology, keeping it working or enabling your dreams to fly on the internet. All are vital to the industry, though our focus here is primarily upon those who provide the tools through which we intend to reach and influence our customers.

> **Most of them are perfectly normal and don't shrivel up at sunrise.**

- The internet is a complicated environment. Unless you are very confident, it is infinitely better to work with those who are masters of it rather than attempt to DIY. Remember that your aims and ambitions can depend on how well you compare with your competitors who are often just one click away – second best is not an option and second chances may not happen.

> **It is infinitely better to work with those who are masters rather than attempt to DIY.**

- **The vast majority** of technical contributors are rather like modern Europeans – progressive, conscientious, well informed and polite enough to automatically switch away from their mother tongue for the benefit of unaccomplished foreign visitors. A tiny few, however, can present a challenge. But there's nothing wrong with geeky, techie or boffish idiosyncrasies if those attributes assist the mission.

> **Being told that your *jugular b.tree fork is giving out a BSOD on the SQL server* is not helpful.**

- **Challenge one:** The most common barrier in the working relationship between techie and non-techie partners is **technical language**. Being told that *your jugular b.tree fork is giving out a BSOD on the SQL server* is not helpful or even relevant to most people. The solution is to stop the conversation at every instance of gobbledegook and request a simplistic translation – but smile warmly as you do so. After several such interruptions the hint will be taken. Think of it as tuning the team to the same wavelength.
- **Challenge two:** Communication is a river that must flow both ways. If the barrier to being understood is **your language** – if your web builder doesn't get what you mean when you ask for a whizzy thing, a twiddley-bit or a thingamabob – then you need to improve your strategy. The simplest remedy is to find similar examples that demonstrate what you want to achieve and show them to your techie. Do also check that what you want is practical, achievable and affordable.
- **Challenge three:** Think of the route to a digital solution as being like a road map. There will be a direct route between A and B, and an array of options that could be better in certain circumstances. Techies delight at options and love debating them. For most of us, this means just one thing – **confusion**. If this happens, stop the conversation and ask your techie to privately consider all the circumstances and filter the options down to just two, together with the pros and cons of each. Reappoint the meeting if necessary and work together to identify the appropriate way forward. Avoid making far-reaching decisions on the hoof.

> **Don't allow your project to become somebody else's testbed.**

- **Challenge four:** Every hour of every day of every week somebody, somewhere, invents a new technical gizmo that is guaranteed to have enthusiastic techies drooling with anticipation. Before you know it your nice, simple, friendly email tool could be festooned with innovative bells and whistles, adding unwanted **complexity**. Don't allow your project to become somebody else's testbed. Never adopt anything new until you've seen it work elsewhere and, above all, have ensured that it enhances the purpose of your project.

- **Challenge five:** It is perhaps unsurprising that some technical providers are on a different **wavelength** to the rest of us. For some, their passion for the predictable logic of computers is infinitely preferable to the complexity and irrationality of people. Sometimes you can find yourself working with somebody who appears shy, reluctant to speak out, remaining on the edge of proceedings and apparently not hard-wired for soft skills. Tread gently and persevere. These folks may be introverted but they often have the answers you need and will open up if encouraged and boosted.
- **Challenge six:** Technical contributors are invariably logic-driven, process thinkers. They excel at numbers and details and are rightly proud of their contribution. Very occasionally (and I do mean VERY occasionally) this technical mastery can seem like technical snobbery. Non-technical contributors complain of being sidelined and diminished. If this happens to you, raise the matter personally and privately.
- **A written brief** with clearly stipulated outcomes and built-in review points will minimise the potential for problems. Personal rapport is an important feature too – language and technical barriers will be less evident if both parties co-operatively pursue a shared objective. The golden guidelines are: be honest if you don't understand; aim to work with a simplifier not a complicator; and be prepared to walk away if the journey becomes uncomfortable.

Summary

Computers and the internet are complex – think twice before you DIY. Skilled technical people are a necessity not an option. If you encounter a language barrier, smile and request a translation. If you own the project expect the provider to use terms you understand. If your own language is inadequate use visual examples to demonstrate your point. Neither request nor permit new or complicated technical tricks unless they serve a useful purpose and are affordable. Aim to work with simplifiers not complicators. Look out for shy boffins and encourage them. Techno-tyrants aside, your project will benefit from different mindset contributions.

Also read sections: 8; 12; 13; 23; 33

45 Working with creatives

'No, don't cry – it's lovely, honestly! Creativity can bring great rewards but care is needed to keep the train on the rails.'

Some years ago, in the corridor of a London Ad agency, I was almost mown down by a long-haired, tie-dyed, gaunt apparition riding a unicycle. I know he was real because he took the trouble to say 'Hi' to me as I dived for cover. Later, I learned he was a photographer, a good one too. One of the joys of working in a creative environment is the opportunity for meeting (and surviving) such characters. Collectively known as 'creatives', these photographers, artists, designers, copywriters and idea-generators see possibilities most of us miss. To succeed, your organisation must stand out from the crowd. This is where creative people are invaluable. Their way of looking at things can add the impact or ideas that get you noticed, understood and remembered.

- Don't be tempted to believe that you can do everything – brilliantly, creatively, originally and effectively – yourself. You can't. There will always be somebody else whose input adds a different dimension that could give your project wings. Creativity should be seen as an aid, not an expense. Creative people should be seen as an extension of your skills pool, not as anomalies (even if some look like they might be). You will get a better result if you make it clear that you value the creative contribution.

There will always be a different dimension that could give your project wings.

- **Everything rides on the brief.** You will invariably get out what you put in. If the brief is confused, overladen or woolly the outcome will be the same. Prepare in advance and talk about where you want to go rather than where you have been. By all means provide background but don't hand over a mountain of information and expect your creative ally to digest it. Aim to brief once. The more you amend your brief the more you risk causing confusion, which could derail both the project and the working relationship. That said, both sides should be prepared for the brief to evolve. The best ideas come from open minds not from those filled with clutter or precast concrete.

The best ideas come from open minds.

- **Set expectations.** There is no reason why SMART principles cannot be adopted by creative providers. Creative minds might sometimes be free-ranging and temperamental but management measures should still apply. Timepaths and budgets stand more chance of working if they are discussed and agreed at the outset. Expect to hold regular update meetings to check progress and direction.

- **Be part of the process.** The mission will benefit if both parties share the journey and a common goal. Though the creative provider might be the specialist contributor you still own the project and can contribute to its outcomes providing you can both agree on the best way forward. There are three things you should avoid: don't get upset if their ideas are better than yours; don't refuse to take part in the process then criticise its every outcome from a distance; and don't reject anything until you understand why it has been done.

- **Never change the team.** More creative projects are wrecked by the introduction of new personalities than by anything else. Any newcomer to a project that is already underway will almost certainty introduce a different agenda. Naturally there are times when this can be desirable, for example if the progress lacks focus or is drifting. Nevertheless, great care should be taken not to throw the baby out with the bath water. Above all, never be tempted to introduce a strictly logical (left brain) thinker into a creative (right brain) process. Having your accountant agonising over the unit cost of pencils is not likely to lubricate outstanding creativity.

Having your accountant agonising over the unit cost of pencils is not likely to lubricate outstanding creativity.

- **Share your vision.** Paint a picture of where you want the project to take you. The more you talk about possibilities the more you will encourage your creative colleagues to begin exploring. Be clear about whether you want an evolution or a revolution – do you just want to move on to the next level or are you seeking a radical solution? Talk about how you want the destination to work for you but try to avoid stipulating exactly how it should be reached – that's their job.

- **Check details.** When appointing a creative resource ask to see examples of their previous work in your field. Also check who will own the intellectual property rights to the work that is produced. Check whether there are any restrictions on what you can do with it once its purpose has been met. For example, some creative originators may expect an additional fee if you use their work in more applications than originally agreed. Some might even expect to retain the original.

- **Committees.** Nothing crushes creativity quicker than a committee, especially one where everyone has a say but nobody has experience of the task at hand. If you want objective progress rather than acrimony and frustration keep the project team as compact and as directly accountable as possible.

Nothing crushes creativity quicker than a committee.

- **Remain objective.** Creativity is a train that gathers momentum quickly and can benefit from subtle (possibly even hidden) control of the brakes. Innovative enthusiasm can get out of hand and set off on a new direction of its own. Sometimes these new tangents can be exciting and highly productive. Good judgement is the only thing that will help you to decide whether to let this new thread unravel or to cut it dead. If in doubt remember that the creative contribution is there to deliver to the aims of the project, not to create new aims of its own.

Summary

Creative wizards who produce magical ideas can give your marketing plans a lift, but there is always a risk that their visionary temperament will clash with the left-brained logic of others, leading your project not into fertile productivity but instead into sulky inertia. Plan in advance, handle ego carefully and show respect for their talents and capabilities. There is no substitute for getting off to the right start: right approach; right brief; right attitude and right management. Creatives may be unconventional – but that's the whole point. Their input can often help turn something average into something outstanding, which is exactly what you want.

Also read sections: 13; 20; 21; 47

46 Hiring consultants

High quality professional advice can provide support, bring progress and create opportunity – but make sure you separate the Pros from the Cons.

Ralph Waldo Emerson expressed the function of consultants generously – '*In every society some are born to rule, and some to advise*'. The advice provided by consultancy will of course change according to circumstances. However, it is reasonably commonplace for an organisation to hire a consultant to provide specialist support in: converting an opportunity; fixing a specific problem; or preparing the way for change. That said, it is conceivable that a consultant might also be appointed to specifically prevent change, as in the case of Leonardo da Vinci who, in 1502, became a consultant to Cesare Borgia, advising on military engineering to ensure that territories owned by Mr Borgia remained that way. Consultants are not rare – Google currently lists more than 11,000 under marketing alone.

High calibre professional guidance which can avoid wasted time and money.

- The Oxford Dictionary defines a consultant as 'A person **qualified to give expert professional advice**, especially a specialist . . .'. Robert Townsend instigated an unfortunate alternative when he labelled consultants as '. . . people who borrow your watch and tell you what time it is, and then walk off with the watch'. However, a more measured view would describe consultants as those capable of providing high calibre professional guidance which, it should be noted, can help avoid wasted time and money.

- Depending on individual style and circumstance, the delivery methods used by a consultant might include: advice; guidance; counselling; advocacy; coaching; and even hands-on management. Consultants are usually outsiders brought into an organisation to assist a specific project or to supplement internal knowledge. Generalist marketing consultants, for example, will provide all-round support and direction, whereas highly specialised providers will focus on specific disciplines including brand development, design, internet strategies, research, web-optimisation and so forth.

- Being a step removed from an organisation's internal issues usually enables a consultant to form **a more objective view** and to avoid (or dismantle) partisan entrenchment. Their professional experience often provides a natural authority, which cuts through inertia and stimulates productive action. Whether the requirement is for industry-specific or issue-specific expertise, the consultant's role is to help (or sometimes cajole) the internal team in identifying then implementing an appropriate response. Some consultants have a background in management and are experienced in handling people as well as operational issues.

- High calibre consultancy professionals can often be sourced **through professional institutes**. Start by contacting *www.cim.co.uk* or *www.ibconsulting.org.uk*. First consider whether you require a consultancy firm or an independent consultant. Use the following criteria for your selection: Does the consultant or consultancy understand your brief? Do they have relevant experience in your sector? Are they capable of dealing with your issue? Is their geographic location convenient? Do they have adequate free time ahead to take the assignment? Does the personal chemistry work both ways? Finally, will their projected fee provide good value?

Does the personal chemistry work both ways?

- Before offering a response your consultant will want to understand your situation. The best way to achieve this will be with a written brief that contains **the salient information**. Two pages will usually be ample. Include background such as: a brief organisational history; the nature of the business and its outputs; the market situation; the kind of customers you have and the ones you'd like to have (if there's a difference); and the general profit or loss situation. Finally, explain the issue as you see it and any other important factors such as timescale, budget and so on.

- Any consultant is likely to have their own method for establishing and understanding the facts so don't be surprised if they ask unexpected questions. It may be that your consultant's proposed solutions might differ from yours. That's what you're paying them for – **a fresh pair of eyes** and an experienced approach. The overarching focus should be on mutually agreed, desired outcomes; the route that the journey might take should be open to debate and development.

Your consultant's proposed solutions might differ from yours. That's what you're paying for.

- Desired outcomes might follow this progression: (1) The problem or issue is defined; (2) The benefits of addressing the issue are also confirmed; (3) The method of approach and component objectives are defined; (4) A detailed plan of action is formed; (5) Required resources – people, equipment, facilities – are agreed; (6) Budget and timescales are set; (7) Measurement criteria are set – regular progress checks and final analysis.

- Lynda Purser, Director of the **Institute of Business Consulting** points out that modern consultancy is not about swooping in and fixing something. It is also very much about encouraging those within the organisation to grow in experience and confidence. They must be part of the journey and not merely passengers on it. The consultant should be the agent of change but not the owner of whatever change brings.

Consultancy is about encouraging those within the organisation to grow in experience and confidence.

- **Wise consultants** will aim to work with and through an organisation's existing management structure, not around it. Taking responsibility for a weak manager is seldom productive and will merely mask a festering problem. A wise consultant will stick to their own skill-sets and will also remain focused entirely on the brief, avoiding the temptation of interfering with peripheral issues. A fully maintained audit trail is sensible, as is Professional Indemnity Insurance.
- At the core of any client and consultant working relationship there should be a **formal contract** – formal meaning written down, but not impenetrably legalistic. Providing both parties agree, this need not amount to any more than one page, providing it includes a clear **definition of agreed deliverables**, payment terms and operational boundaries. The way you choose and manage your consultants is crucial to the success of the assignment.

Summary

Consultants can operate as independent specialist workers or as part of a multifunctional consultancy firm. They are usually brought in to provide advice or guidance on a specific situation – sometimes a problem, sometimes an opportunity. Their external positioning usually gives a consultant a fresh perspective on internal issues and potential barriers. Consultants may have a management background and be experienced in people issues as well as operational issues. Many consultants are members of professional institutes and can be found on professional directories. The starting point for choosing a consultant is usually an outline brief. Consultancy can be as much about facilitating confidence as providing specialist advice.

Also read sections: 1; 2; 7; 8; 13

47 Hiring freelancers

'Commerce is blessed with a ready supply of talented soloists who can help your orchestra to extend its repertoire.'

We Brits make keen freelancers, prepared to accept insecurity for the benefit of being our own boss. According to the Professional Contractors' Group, 14 per cent of UK professionals work for themselves, while in the US the corresponding figure is 7.5 per cent. A curious feature of freelance workers is their apparent immunity from common ailments, of the sort that sometimes prevent salaried staff from attending work. Interesting freelance notables include Christopher Columbus, an Italian paid by the Spanish to go and find India – he missed and found America instead – and Attila the Hun, who took money from the Romans for being nice but later decided to set up in the empire business for himself. Fortunately, the freelance workers who inhabit the marketing industry are generally more reliable.

- A freelance is an **independent, self-employed professional specialist** or contractor. In the context of marketing this can include graphic designers, copywriters, retouchers, illustrators, media buyers, web-developers, researchers, et al. They commonly operate on an hourly, daily or project fee basis and take care of their own tax and business overheads. Freelancers earn more than salaried staff but cost less to hire than a full-service agency.

- Freelance providers are usually hired for their specialist skill or to temporarily fill a gap within the in-house team, perhaps during busy periods or as holiday cover. They can also provide **a flexible solution** for organisations in a growth curve that have not yet reached a level that justifies extra permanent staff. Most freelancers are able to work in-house at the client's premises, though the growing impact of the internet offers 24/7 flexibility.

- The freelance rationale varies. Some have become freelance as a last resort, due to redundancy for example, some have chosen the pathway because it offers the opportunity for more flexibility or more money, more status, more variety or, more control. Sensible freelancers appreciate that they will only win regular business if they do a good job and add value. Consequently most will **'go the extra mile'** (though some might add

> **Freelancers invariably spend less time off sick and more time at work.**

it to the bill). Freelancers invariably spend less time off sick and more time at work than salaried staff.

- **Potential pitfalls** include: a freelancer's skill might be limited to a single specialised focus; there could be issues of trust and confidentiality, both in terms of how much freelancers learn about your organisation and about how close they get (or might be tempted to get) to your clients; whether or not they bear a legal liability for errors or consequential effects. The most consistent gripe from patrons is that service continuity can be disrupted if the freelance is juggling the needs of several clients simultaneously.

- **On the plus side**, most freelance providers are highly experienced and often at the top of their profession (cheeky student blaggers please note). They are used to addressing the most challenging roles in strained circumstances and can frequently introduce you to a useful network of colleagues. Serious freelancers have a mature business attitude (cheeky student blaggers – note 2) and expect to provide solid service at a sensible price – after all their livelihood depends on regular commissions. Beyond helping you get the job done freelance workers are usually easy and uncomplicated to employ and generate less administrative burden than full-time staff.

> **Most freelance providers are highly experienced and often at the top of their profession.**

- **On the part of the client**, a mindset shift is sometimes required for the relationship to work. Be prepared to have to explain things in more detail, remember that the freelance will not automatically know how your operation works or what it expects. Be prepared also to spend more of your own time managing the project, or the freelancer, than would routinely be the case. Importantly, remember that freelance workers are independent – they are not your regular staff and may exercise their liberty to walk away if you behave like a tyrant. Freelancers arriving at your premises will need to be shown where things are and given appropriate induction into health and safety matters and emergency procedures.

> **Freelance workers may exercise their liberty to walk away if you behave like a tyrant.**

- **Before appointing a freelance** always ask to see examples of previous work and perhaps even talk to past patrons. It is wise to test the relationship on a small project to begin with. Most pitfalls can be avoided if both parties think the project through beforehand and state their respective expectations. Consider the need for a written contract to confirm the agreed price, possible extra expenses, delivery dates, working hours, continuity, roles and responsibilities, payment terms and the ownership of intellectual property rights. Regular update meetings should be held as the project progresses.

- If you find a useful freelance impress them by paying promptly. Having the payment notification for project one waiting on their desk when they arrive for project two scores every time. Because of their flexible, nomadic nature freelancers can be a valuable source of information on how things are done elsewhere. This can be a helpful benefit but beware, the tide of information can flow both ways. To reduce the potential for damage consider a confidentiality agreement as part of each project.

Having the payment for project one waiting when they arrive for project two scores every time.

- Well-prepared freelance contributors might have a Professional Indemnity Policy to cover against errors and omissions (cheeky student blaggers – note 3). They will also have the courtesy to check with you before using your project in their samples portfolio (note 4!). Those appointing freelance providers will be delighted to learn that the legal onus is on you to ensure that those you hire are **genuine, self-employed professionals**, not terrorists or moonlighters.

Summary

They'll cost more than your regular staff but less than an agency. Often they are specialists and can be drafted in to fill a gap in your team. They hire themselves out by the hour, by the day, or by the duration of the contract. Freelancers work in-house or alternatively might contribute via the internet. They get sick less often than staff and they probably put in more effort but, ultimately, they can leave when they want and could take your secrets with them. By and large they are a helpful and flexible solution and an excellent source of experience, knowledge and contacts. Always agree fees and expectations in advance.

Also read sections: 12; 13; 46; 49

48 Buying print

Reports of the death of the print industry may have been exaggerated. The possibilities for paper and ink remain alive and well.

The innovation of the printing press changed the destiny of mankind. Now, five and a half centuries later, further technological leaps have transformed the printing industry. It is now possible to print just one or two copies of an entire book economically or to print huge vinyl sheets that will cover an entire building. Such advancements have not been without cost and many traditional providers have fallen by the wayside. Interestingly, the one much-heralded change that failed to materialise with the incoming tide of technology was the paperless society. Despite the enchantments of the internet it seems that our tactile affinity with paper remains popular. If you are new to buying printing services it would be wise to familiarise yourself with the basics before taking the plunge.

- **Print is a horses-for-courses game.** Large web-offset machines specialising in churning vast quantities of magazines would not be suitable for business stationery. Similarly, your local Business Print and Copy shop might not be the best choice for exhibition stand panels. Look for the right horse and always ask for a written quotation. If you ask more than one provider to quote, make sure that you give each contender the same written 'brief'. This will help you to obtain and evaluate comparative estimates.

- **Look for a printer who thinks beyond** the production of the job and considers your holistic needs or limits. If your organisation is contemplating a major design exercise, which will result in significant print work, industry experts Leo Print suggest you consider also inviting the printer to comment on the practical aspects of the project. This can often save both money and bloodshed further down the track.

> **Inviting the printer to comment on the practical aspects of the project can save both money and bloodshed.**

- Print professionals are invariably helpful, knowledgeable and adept at finding different ways of skinning the same cat. This can often save you time, trouble and money, so **be prepared to listen** to their advice. Alternatively, you could hand your print sourcing and buying needs to a print broker who will use their own trade contacts to get the results you want. They will also negotiate costs directly with the printer then add their own commission. Similarly, graphic designers will usually organise printing for you, though they will be keener if they designed and produced that which is to be printed.

- Once you have a written quotation feel at liberty to clarify anything that you don't understand. It is much better for both parties to address any concerns at this stage rather than further down the line. When you place your order, especially if using email, make sure you receive an acknowledgement. Check that the details match your requirement. Also check completion dates and delivery dates are appropriate.

- Unless the print job is an exact repeat of a previous project, always **arrange for a proof** copy that you can check and approve before the final run. The proof stage should be seen as an opportunity to check colours and technical details, not as an extended opportunity to rewrite all your text or alter the design. Always check proofs carefully even if it takes time to do so. Remember you will have to sign-off the proof and confirm that you are happy to proceed. If you change your mind beyond this point it could be expensive.

If you change your mind beyond this point it could be expensive.

- Minor amendments made at the proof stage are often carried out free of charge. However, you should bear in mind that there may be an additional charge for new proofs. Always check this point prior to requesting alterations. Major changes will almost certainly be chargeable.

- Where possible, avoid printing any **information that might change in the future** – such as addresses, telephone numbers or people's names – in four colour (CMYK). It will help reduce potential revision costs if all such information is printed in black. That is, unless the job has been produced using digital techniques where the cost of colour is not an issue. Advances in digital print have revolutionised the industry and given rise to many possibilities. For example, direct mail, leaflets, brochures and even books can now be fully personalised to individually named recipients.

Advances in digital print have revolutionised the industry and given rise to many possibilities.

- **It costs as much** to set up a traditional printing press for three copies as for 3,000 copies. If you want to print in small quantities you will probably be better off looking for a printer with a digital press. Alternatively, if your requirement is for frequent or large runs you could investigate in-house production using machines that are more like large photocopiers than printing presses. These will enable you to control the project yourself – and of course the cost. But, inevitably, you will encounter other expenses for capital equipment, consumables and possibly operators' salaries.

- If you are asked to pay some of your **print costs in advance** (not uncommon for first time customers) it might be wise to first make some gentle enquiries about the financial stability of the print company before you hand over funds. The sudden closure of any supplier, printer or otherwise, who holds your job or your money will hurt.
- Because it is the final operation at the end of a chain of other operations the print function is almost **always squeezed for time**. Anything that reduces the leeway for errors has a knack of tempting fate and risking catastrophe, for which the printer is usually blameless. The best safeguard is simply not to leave it until the last minute.

The best safeguard is simply not to leave it until the last minute.

Summary

Do: avoid anyone who tries to bamboozle you with jargon; get fresh eyes to check proofs; pay particular attention to names, numbers and addresses; proofread working from the bottom up – this finds mistakes more reliably; be aware that you might have to pay for any error that comes to light after the proof is signed-off – whether it is your mistake or not; check if delivery costs are included; store paper stock flat and away from damp or heat. Don't expect the printer to write brilliant text or to advise your marketing strategy – that's not their job. Remember to retrieve your artwork originals when the job is complete.

Also read sections: 12; 20; 21; 22; 42

49 Negotiating

'Whether you're a buyer, a seller or an employee you can either accept what you get or negotiate to get what you want.'

Not all negotiations are about suppliers and clients or buying and selling. Nor are they always about pitching for a deal. For example, you could find yourself using common negotiation techniques with colleagues to agree how to best manage a project or even to avoid holiday roster clashes. Wise managers see negotiation as an opportunity to reach an agreement that enables everyone to move forward and, above all, to strengthen a productive relationship so that it will last rather than become an unproductive cul-de-sac. Inevitably, some negotiations stall, end in unhappy compromise or else with an agreement not to agree at all. The only certainty is that the better prepared you are, the more chance you have of achieving what you want.

- **Arrive in good time**, be alert, focused, in control and relaxed. Prepare to be surprised, challenged, even bullied, but know that these are merely tactics. Providing you anticipate them, you can rise above them. Adopt a positive attitude but be prepared to be flexible.

Prepare to be surprised, challenged, even bullied.

- **Consider in advance** what your ideal outcome will be and see this as your final fallback position – aim to use the negotiation process to improve on it. Open the bidding with a degree of audacity to test the other side. Also decide in advance (but don't disclose) what your main goal is and what you are prepared to concede to reach it (and at what point you will walk away if you can't). Neither expect nor agree to a split-the-difference situation, unless it works in your favour.
- **Where possible**, control the environment. For example, avoid seating positions that might diminish your confidence and avoid positions where peripheral activity might distract you. You should never assume that the other side will play the same game as you – they might not be as open, honest and ethical as you or as closed, dishonest and unethical as you (delete as applicable).

Avoid positions that might diminish your confidence.

- **Control your body language.** Use open friendly gestures, keep eye contact, remain polite and smile. Looking relaxed and confident is an advantage. Don't talk unless there's something important to say – if you're talking you're not listening. Keep your hands away from your face. Avoid words and phrases that might betray uncertainty. For example, use 'What I need from you is . . .' rather than 'In an ideal world, what I'd be grateful for, if at all possible . . .' Remain professional and controlled. Don't become offensive, choose your words carefully, stick to the issues and avoid personal put-downs or point scoring.

- **Before attempting to negotiate**, confirm the requirements of the other side. Write a list and get them to agree that it represents their aims. If you get this out in the open early you can see exactly what you are dealing with and prevent each separate requirement being used later to ratchet further concessions. Pick-off the easy issues at the start of the discussion. This will help both parties to find common ground and build a platform for co-operative progress towards the bigger issues.
- **Never pre-negotiate.** Don't offer any concessions until the other side gives a firm agreement to do business. If they don't intend to deal in the first place you will only undermine yourself by trying. When matters do begin to move you should not accept the first offer that's made because it will set a precedent. Similarly, when you have to give ground do so in smaller increments than the other side expect. Never give ground without gaining something in return. For example, 'I can squeeze the price a little more, but I'll need quick payment to justify it.'
- **Buyers will normally try** to get the seller to make the first significant bid because they know that the side that opens the bidding usually carries the disadvantage. Be realistic about what you might be able to achieve – buyers can (and will) usually walk away more readily than sellers unless the offering is very special. Buyers will often try to diminish the value of the offering, sometimes chipping away just a little at a time. The seller can counter this by having a few killer benefits in reserve.

The side that opens the bidding usually carries the disadvantage.

- **Avoid the automatic** bid-followed-by-counter-bid situation. It can be more useful to interrupt the predictable flow, restate your position and throw the onus back to the other side, inviting them to rethink their last bid. If you need to buy time to think try deferring to a superior. For example, 'I don't think my boss will agree to that, but I'm keen to do business – I'll step outside now and make a call'.

- **Summarise points of agreement** aloud and in writing as the meeting proceeds. Ensure that the other side endorses them. This will help prevent backsliding. When you sense that a deal is near, it's important not to rush the last few fences. Keep one final benefit or concession up your sleeve in case you need some last minute leverage.
- Once you've tabled your closing offer remain silent. Don't feel obliged to qualify it or explain yourself. Use the pounding silence to pile pressure onto the other side. When the deal is done, get the all important handshake (AKA irreversible moral commitment) as soon as possible and congratulate the other side. Providing you get more or less what you want, there's no harm in letting them feel that they won too. But do watch out for the final nibble just as your hand reaches for the doorknob and when your guard is down.

Watch out for the final nibble as your hand reaches for the doorknob.

Summary

Either you accept what you are given or you negotiate to get what you want. One option will do more for your self-esteem – not to mention your bank balance – than the other. But remember that negotiation need not be about achieving a crushing victory. It is also a means of settling day-to-day working procedures and building rather than destroying productive relationships. Ultimately, negotiation is about agreeing terms for finding a way forward. Remember too that there is an optimum time to negotiate – preferably while you have leverage. If you remember nothing else never forget that post-event negotiation doesn't work.

Also read sections: 7; 8; 13; 24

CHAPTER EIGHT

The point of it all – profitable customers

In this chapter:

50 Happy customers

> *The good, the bad and the hideous, where would your organisation and its ambitions be without customers?*

That old addage – never have a customer you can't afford to lose – is sensible advice. If you have just one key client you could lose your integrity and your freedom but should they defect you could lose a whole lot more! The number of customers you have, or intend to have, should be something that is arrived at by choice, not something that is left to happenstance. And it should be related to both your organisation's ambitions and its capacity to manage. Having more customers than you can cope with is equally as questionable as the automatic assumption that growth is a necessity. What of those customers you already have? What do they think of you? Are you assuming all is joyful? Is it time for some questions?

- **What do you want from your customers?** You will want three things. You will want your customers to be satisfied as a result of their involvement with your organisation. You will want them to return and buy from you again in the future. You will want to be certain that your organisation profited from the transaction.

- **What do you REALLY want?** If you are part of an organisation with an appetite for growth you will want more customers and more profit to fuel your ambition. Or, you might be a contented soloist who wants for nothing more than to earn a reasonable living and enjoy control over your working life. In which case, you will be more interested in acquiring selected customers rather than masses. Both options are perfectly fine. What is important is that you consider the question rather than act or react blindly. Business growth is an attainable option for some – not an obligation for all.

> **Every single customer of your business wants you to understand one stupidly crucial thing.**

- **What do customers want from you?** Every single customer of your business wants you to understand one stupidly crucial thing – that there is no such thing as an average customer. You might have to think of them in large numbers when planning to capture their hearts and minds, but the day they catch you treating them like sheep in a flock rather than as genuinely valued individuals could be the beginning of the end. Each customer you have has a name, a personality, wants, needs and worries. The closer you can get to treating them as real people the better.

- **Are they always right?** If you cannot afford to lose or offend a single customer then there are just two rules for you to observe: Rule 1 – the customer IS always right. Even if they have three heads, lie through their teeth and are wrong – they are right! Rule 2 – if you hate them, can prove them wrong and want to vaporise them – defer to Rule 1.

If you hate them, can prove them wrong and want to vaporise them – defer to Rule 1.

- **Are customers ever wrong?** Yes, though not because of their position on a particular issue, but because they can sometimes be completely ill-suited to the needs of the business. Of course, a business exists to meet the needs of its customers, but its foremost duty is to itself and those within it. Customers who do not fit the target segments, or whose demands exceed their value or who otherwise divert the organisation from its course are 'wrong'. Rule 3 – customers can be fired too. Those who hijack the ambitions of the business are wrong – ignore Rule 1.

Customers who hijack the ambitions of the business are wrong – ignore Rule 1.

- **Should some customers matter more?** Big customers, bulk buyers, key accounts, regulars – these groups can give a business solidarity and substance. You will want to encourage them to stick with you, to be lifetime buyers rather than casuals or one-offs. Make sure you provide them with incentives that make it clear that you value them. Spoil them (make sure that they notice), spend time with them and say thank you occasionally.

- **Should you check your performance?** Taking regular soundings, measuring customer satisfaction, monitoring competitor activity, evaluating the number of returning customers – all standard marketing practice. Most unhappy customers just go, you don't always get the chance to make amends if something goes wrong. It is much easier, not to mention more effective, to seek feedback routinely.

- **Are complaints bad?** An angry customer could simply have walked away. The fact that they are complaining gives you a chance to put things right AND to learn where your organisation needs to improve. Complaints are therefore potentially positive. Standard steps are: (1) Calm the anger. Empathise, talk quietly and remain controlled.

(2) Tell the complainant that you want to hear them out and that you want to put things right – but also that they need to be calm before the process can begin. (3) Don't apologise for any error or wrong-doing until you know what it is or was. (4) Establish what it will take to settle the problem – ask the complainant to be specific. (5) If you can provide what they want then do. If you can't, be honest but firm – then offer appropriate alternatives. (6) Accept that you might not always win.

- **Who else needs to know?** There's no point in the sales team doing a great job if the delivery guys mess up. There's no point in having fantastic flight attendants if the customer's baggage gets lost. There's no point in having a whizzy online ordering facility if the shoes that arrive are the wrong size. Customer care cannot happen only in selective parts of your organisation, it must work all the way through.

There's no point in having fantastic flight attendants if the customer's baggage gets lost.

Summary

Customers are important. Acquiring them in the right numbers and looking after them properly requires consideration, not auto-assumptions. You will want your customers to be satisfied, to return and to furnish profit. You will also want them to complement, not confound, your ambitions. Customers do not wish to be seen as 'average'. Under-promise but over-deliver. Avoid customer contact systems when you could user customer contact. If growth by sheer numbers is what you want then every customer IS always right, they are only wrong if they affect the trajectory of the organisation. Take regular soundings, make sure that customer care runs all the way through your organisation.

Also read sections: 6; 7; 12; 19; 38

Index

Notes

Notes